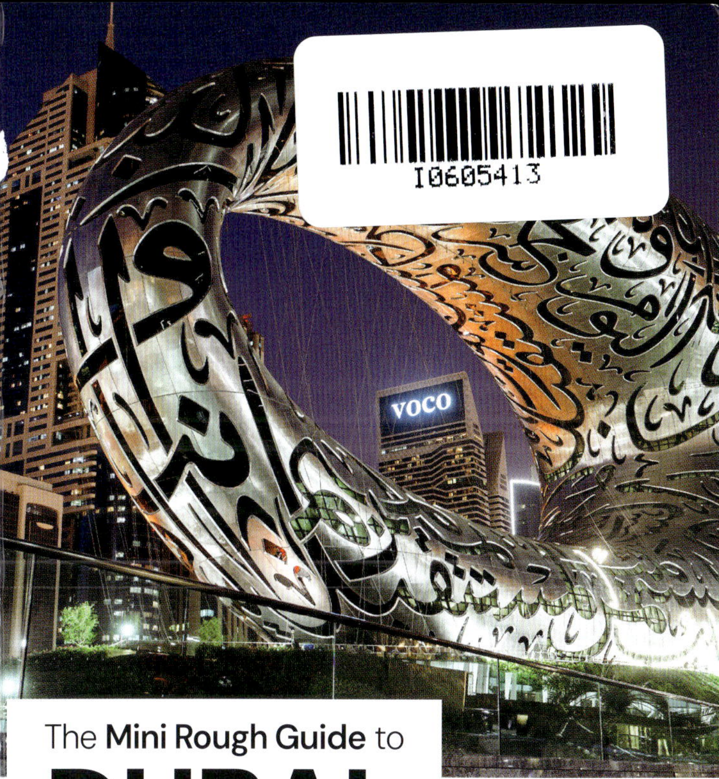

The **Mini Rough Guide** to

DUBAI

YOUR TAILOR-MADE TRIP STARTS HERE

HOW ROUGHGUIDES.COM/TRIPS WORKS

STEP 1

Pick your dream destination, tell us what you want and submit an enquiry.

STEP 2

Fill in a short form to tell your local expert about your dream trip and preferences.

STEP 3

Our local expert will craft your tailor-made itinerary. You'll be able to tweak and refine it until you're completely satisfied.

STEP 4

Book online with ease, pack your bags and enjoy the trip! Our local expert will be on hand 24/7 while you're on the road.

PLAN AND BOOK YOUR TRIP AT ROUGHGUIDES.COM/TRIPS

How to download your Free eBook

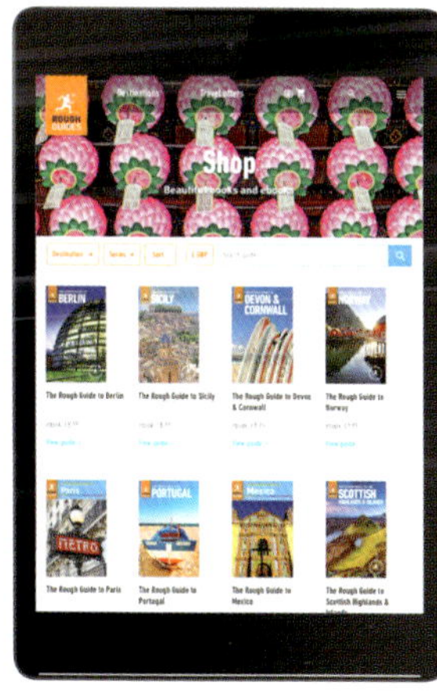

1. Visit **www.roughguides.com/free-ebook** or scan the **QR code** opposite

2. Enter the code **dubai665**
3. Follow the simple step-by-step instructions

For troubleshooting contact: mail@roughguides.com

Contents

Introduction

Nowhere is quite like Dubai. In barely five decades, the city has transformed itself from a modest Arabian trading town, which few outside the region had ever heard of, into one of the planet's most glamorous, futuristic destinations, home to the world's tallest building, its biggest shopping mall, its largest man-made island and a host of other spectacular, record-busting developments.

For some, modern Dubai is one of the twenty-first century's great urban experiments; an attempt to create a truly global city and become one of the world's essential destinations. For others it is frequently seen as a panegyric to consumerist luxury: a self-indulgent haven of magical hotels, superlative restaurants and extravagantly themed malls. Perhaps not surprisingly the city is often stereotyped as appealing only to those with more cash than culture, although this one-eyed cliché does no justice to Dubai's beguiling contrasts and rich cultural make-up. The city's headline-grabbing mega-projects have also deflected attention from Dubai's role in providing the Islamic world with a model of political stability and religious tolerance, showing what can be achieved by a peaceful and progressive regime in one of the planet's most turbulent regions.

Inside the Museum of the Future

WHAT'S NEW

With new exhibition spaces still being added, **Al Shindagha Museum** in the old city is Dubai's most ambitious cultural project to date, transforming swathes of Shindagha into the definitive repository of Emirati culture, crafts and history. At the opposite end of the city, the vast Expo 2020 site is now being repurposed as **Expo City Dubai** district, preserving many of the Expo's headline attractions including the stunning Al Wasl Plaza and the aptly named "Surreal" fountain, whose waters really do flow uphill. Sort of. Other new landmarks include the superyacht-styled **Jumeirah Marsa Al Arab** mega-resort, sitting alongside the *Burj Al Arab*, and the **Atlantis Royal** resort, looking like a huge pile of bricks balanced precariously on the edge of The Palm, while the funky new **J1 Beach** complex in Jumeirah offers one of the city's ultimate chill-out spaces. And don't miss the wacky **Museum of the Future**, a huge, squashed doughnut covered in calligraphic swirls which has already established itself as one of the city's weirdest and most wonderful sights.

For the visitor, there's far more to Dubai than designer boutiques and five-star hotels – although of course if all you're looking for is a luxurious dose of sun, sand and shopping, the city can't be beaten. If you want to step beyond the tourist clichés, however, you'll find so much more on offer, from the fascinating old city centre, with its labyrinth of bustling souks interspersed with fine old traditional Arabian houses, to the memorably quirky architectural landmarks of the modern city. Dubai's human geography is no less memorable, featuring a cosmopolitan assortment of Emiratis, Arabs, Iranians, Indians, Filipinos and Europeans – a fascinating patchwork of peoples and languages that gives the city its uniquely varied cultural appeal. Twenty-five years on from the opening of the iconic *Burj Al Arab*, Dubai shows no signs of slowing down, and with new mega-projects announced on an almost annual basis the city remains one of the most fascinating and vibrant places to visit.

A summer day in Dubai

DUBAI PAST AND PRESENT

Modern Dubai's go-for-it dynamism is nothing new and the city has always boasted an entrepreneurial spirit and a willingness to seize whatever opportunities it has been presented with. As early as 1894, Sheikh Maktoum bin Hasher al Maktoum was enticing merchants from Iran and India to settle in the city with the promise of zero taxation, establishing the basis of the modern city's cosmopolitan and business-friendly outlook. Old Dubai was a flourishing port long before oil was discovered in the emirate in 1966, at various times making a living out of a vibrant trade in pearls and gold, as well as other commercial activities.

The development of the modern city was kick-started by the discovery of oil in the 1960s (although Dubai's oil reserves have only ever been relatively modest and now account for barely one percent of the emirate's GDP, unlike its oil-rich neighbour, Abu Dhabi). Oil revenues provided the funds to construct a modern industrial infrastructure, supervised by the canny Sheikh Rashid, who laid the foundations for the city's current prosperity. Sheikh Mohammed, Rashid's son and the current ruler of Dubai, further accelerated the pace of diversification, overseeing the construction of lavish tourist facilities alongside a string of business-friendly initiatives ranging from assorted free-trade and financial zones aimed at positioning

Dubai as the tourist, business and financial capital of the Middle East. Foreigners now outnumber native Emiratis by more than ten to one, giving the city its extremely multicultural and cosmopolitan flavour, with the overall population of around 3.3 million including citizens from just about every country in the world.

Not surprisingly, there have been growing pains along the way. Exploitation and alleged human-rights abuses of low-paid Indian and Pakistani construction workers have regularly blighted the city's image, while environmental concerns associated with Dubai's various mega-developments are another issue. Social tensions between the many different nationalities cohabiting within the city also continue to provoke friction, while the regular incarceration of visiting Westerners on charges ranging from carrying drugs to kissing in public has generated endless critical column inches overseas.

WHEN TO GO

Easily the best time to visit Dubai is during the cooler winter months (December to February), when the city enjoys a pleasantly Mediterranean climate, with average daily temperatures in the mid-20s°C. Not surprisingly, room rates (and demand) are at their peak during these months, although skies in January and February can sometimes be rather overcast, and it can even rain, sometimes quite heavily. Temperatures rise significantly through March and April, though the heat is still relatively bearable and shouldn't stop you getting out and about. October is similarly hot, with temperatures falling through November.

During the summer months (May to September) the city transforms into a veritable furnace – July and August are especially suffocating – with average temperatures in the high 30s to low 40s, or even higher, staying punishingly hot even after dark. In compensation, room rates at many hotels plummet by as much as 75 percent, making this an excellent time to enjoy some authentic Dubaian luxury at bargain prices, assuming you're happy to stick to air-conditioned hotels, shopping malls, restaurants and clubs.

WHAT TO SEE

Modern Dubai's attempt to conquer the global tourist market is based on a wide range of purpose-built attractions, although the main draw for many visitors is simply the city's almost uninterrupted year-round sunshine, with plenty of beaches to choose from and fancy hotel pools to lounge beside. If you're here simply to chill and indulge, then Dubai has spectacular spas and shopping, and some of the Middle East's best eating, drinking and clubbing.

Scratch the surface, however, and there's a lot more to Dubai than you might imagine. Many visitors are surprised by the old city's palpable sense of history, with its traditional Iranian-style wind-tower houses, bustling covered souks and stately old dhows ploughing serenely down the waters of the Creek. You could easily spend a day or two here, especially if you visit the vast new Al Shindagha Museum, the city's most ambitious cultural project to date.

Burj Khalifa, the world's tallest building

It's Dubai's record-breaking modern attractions, however, which have really captured the global imagination. The iconic, sail-shaped *Burj Al Arab* more or less single-handedly put Dubai on the map back in the noughties. Since then, the city has added the world's tallest building, largest shopping mall, biggest fountain and a host of other showstoppers – not to mention the Palm Jumeirah, one of the world's

EMIRATI DRESS

Most Emirati nationals wear UAE national dress in the workplace, at home and when out and about. For men this comprises a white, floor-length robe known as the *kandoora* or *dishdasha* plus a cloth headdress (*gutra*) secured by a stiff black cord known as an *agal*, with which the Emiratis' *bedu* ancestors hobbled their camels' legs – although baseball caps are Increasingly replacing the *gutra* and *agal* among young men. Women traditionally dress in a floor-length black cloak (*abaya*) plus headscarf (*sheyla*). Older women may be seen wearing the stiff gold and lacquer face mask known as a *burqa*, though this is increasingly rare except out in rural back-waters. Children are often dressed in Western-style clothes.

largest artificial islands. But it's the sheer speed and scale of the development which really takes the breath away, most notably in the futuristic Dubai Marina development, which transformed in little over five years from empty desert into a forest of bristling skyscrapers, now home to the densest concentration of high-rises on the planet. Even now Dubai continues to open up major new attractions on a seemingly annual basis, with recent additions including the wonderfully outlandish Museum of the Future, the superyacht-inspired *Marsa Al Arab* hotel and the state-of-the-art architectural curiosities built for the Expo 2020.

Away from the city itself, the desert is a major draw for many visitors, and few people turn down the chance to experience one of the ever-popular "sunset safaris". Longer and more meaningful sand excursions can also be arranged, perhaps with a visit to the beautiful Dubai Desert Conservation Reserve en route, where you can see some of Arabia's original and most endangered fauna. Other rewarding day-trips include visits to the staid neighbouring emirate of Sharjah, home to a several excellent museums, or further afield to the oasis garden city of Al Ain or to Abu Dhabi, the capital of the United Arab Emirates (UAE) with a further slew of major attractions.

LAYOUT OF THE CITY

Dubai is the second largest of the seven emirates which make up the UAE. Located northeast of the federal capital, Abu Dhabi, on the southern shore of the Arabian Gulf, Dubai faces Iran and covers 4,114 sq km (1,588 sq miles) of flat coastal plain and rolling desert dunes, with the barren Hajar mountains in the east around the Dubai enclave of Hatta, which is physically separated from the rest of the Dubai emirate.

The modern city is extremely linear, stretching for over 25km (15 miles) from the old city districts down to Dubai Marina and Jebel Ali. Multi-lane Sheikh Zayed Road runs the length of the city, connecting the various districts and continuing to Abu Dhabi. Most of the city's major tourist attractions lie on or within a few kilometres of the glittering, sun-drenched coast, with almost everywhere easily reachable using the city's state-of-the-art metro and tram systems

Train entering the station with Dubai's high-rises in the background

Lying on either side of the Creek, the districts of **Bur Dubai** and **Deira** form the heart of the old city, as well as the hub of the metro and bus systems. South and west of here the suburbs of **Karama**, **Oud Metha** and **Garhoud** are mementos of the city's early expansion back in the 1960s and 70s, and also home to a few further attractions.

SUSTAINABLE TRAVEL

The city's excellent **public transport** network goes pretty much everywhere, and there are plenty of bikes for hire too, plus many miles of dedicated cycle track (see page 101). For **accommodation**, check out the list of Green Globe-certified establishments at www.greenglobe.com. In terms of **eating**, stick to local produce if you can. Fish served straight from the boat in the cheap seafood restaurants of Jumeirah is a great option, while dishes at local Arabian cafés and curry houses are also likely to have a relatively low food mileage. Or, try one of the city's three restaurants boasting the coveted Michelin "Green" Star (see page 108). Avoid buying endless disposable plastic **water bottles** and bring your own refillable bottle to top up as you go. The new "Dubai Can" scheme (www.visitdubai.com/en/dubai-can) offers convenient free refills at over thirty locations. The jewel in Dubai's **conservation** crown is undoubtedly the **Dubai Desert Conservation Reserve** (see page 88). Stereotypical desert safaris (see page 98) are a lot less eco-friendly. Choose an eco-conscious operator such as Arabian Adventures (www.arabian-adventures.com) or Platinum Heritage (www.platinum-heritage.com).

South of Karama, the modern city really gets going in earnest with the massed skyscrapers of **Sheikh Zayed Road**, which march south to the **Downtown Dubai** development and the mighty **Burj Khalifa**. From here, it's a relatively short hop back to the coast, where you'll find the city's best stretch of beach and a landmark cluster of buildings including the famous **Burj Al Arab** and the **Madinat Jumeirah**.

Continuing south brings you to the turn off to the **Palm Jumeirah** artificial island and, shortly afterwards, to the towers of the **Dubai Marina** development. Beyond here yet more development is underway, with the gradual opening of the vast new Dubai World airport and Expo City Dubai, in the far south of the city, close to the border with Abu Dhabi emirate.

10 Things not to miss

1 **BURJ AL ARAB**
This "seven-star" hotel is the city's architectural icon. See page 71.

2 **SHEIKH ZAYED ROAD**
Home to a futuristic array of soaring skyscrapers plus the remarkable Museum of the Future. See page 56.

3 **THE GOLD SOUK**
Pick up a glittering souvenir of Dubai in this world-famous shopping quarter. See page 46.

4 **AL FAHIDI**
Traditional wind-tower houses are the attraction in the city's restored historic quarter. See page 42.

5 **MALL TIME**
Max out your credit cards at Dubai's dazzling array of shopping malls. See page 60.

6 **ABRAS (WATER TAXIS)**
Enjoy a ride between the traditional souks on either side of Dubai Creek. See page 45.

7 **DESERT SAFARI**
Head out into the desert for an exhilarating 4x4 ride across the dunes. See page 140.

8 **MADINAT JUMEIRAH**
A fabulous re-creation of old Arabia, with souks, restaurants, cafés and canals. See page 73.

9 **SHEIKH ZAYED MOSQUE**
This Abu Dhabi landmark is one of the world's largest and most opulent mosques. See page 91.

10 **DOWNTOWN DUBAI**
A clutch of record-breaking attractions centred on the extraordinary Burj Khalifa, the world's tallest building. See page 59.

A perfect day in Dubai

9.00AM

Gold and spices. After breakfast in your hotel, head to the glittering Gold Souk in Deira, exploring the gold shops and adjacent Spice Souk.

11.00AM

Historical interlude. Hop on an abra for the five-minute ride across the Creek to Bur Dubai and then spend some time exploring the excellent Al Shindagha Museum – an essential point of reference for anyone interested in the city's history and culture.

1.00PM

Wind towers. Head down to the atmospheric Al Fahidi Historical Neighbourhood, with its marvellous old wind-towered houses, and grab a bite to eat at the beautiful *XVA Café* and gallery.

2.00PM

Into the new city. Catch a cab or take the metro for the short journey south to the spectacular skyscrapers of Sheikh Zayed Road. Get out at the iconic Emirates Tower and walk down the strip, admiring the remarkable Museum of the Future and eclectic high-rise architecture en route.

2.30PM

Shopping. From the bottom of Sheikh Zayed Road catch a cab (or take the metro) to the Dubai Mall. Spend some time here browsing the shops and perhaps visiting the in-house aquarium.

3.30PM

Up to the top. Exit through the back of the Dubai Mall to reach the heart of the Downtown Dubai development, with the Dubai Fountain in front of you and the huge Burj Khalifa, the world's tallest building, to your right. Head into the Burj and ride a high-speed elevator up to the At The Top observation deck for sweeping views of the city.

4.30PM

Sail of the century. Catch a cab and head down to the stunning Madinat Jumeirah complex, explore the Madinat's souk, canals and shops, and then enjoy the unforgettable views of the sail-shaped *Burj Al Arab* next door over a sundowner at the *Bahri Bar*.

7.00PM

Arabian night. There is a vast range of superb places to eat all around the Madinat Jumeirah – the canalside venues are particularly lively after dark and a great place to people- watch. After dinner, catch a tram for the short trip up to the *One&Only Royal Mirage* hotel and head to the gorgeous little *Rooftop Bar*, which often has a DJ later on.

Dubai for foodies

9.00AM

Arabian breakfast. Start the day with a classic Arabian-style breakfast at *Al Khayma Heritage Restaurant* in Al Fahidi – try the lavish "Emirati breakfast try" including *balalit* vermicelli noodles and crispy *regag* flatbread.

10.30AM

Spice Souk. Walk through Bur Dubai souk and catch an abra over to Deira to browse the wonderful array of spices and teas in the fragrant Spice Souk. Then head up to the adjacent Gold Souk for a reviving cut of masala chai from one of the Indian cafés tucked away in the surrounding alleyways and perhaps a refreshing scoop of genuine camel-milk ice cream from the *Geewin* kiosk at the western entrance to the souk.

11.30AM

Food shopping in Burjuman. Catch the metro back to the Burjuman centre and pick up some gourmet Saudi Arabian dates from the upmarket Bateel shop. Then dive into the adjacent Carrefour hypermarket. It's not the most atmospheric place to shop, but the range of local foodstuffs on offer, from traditional spice mixes to Yemeni honey, can't be beaten, and prices are the cheapest in the city.

1.30PM

Lunch by the sea. Head south to the Jumeirah Fish Market and lunch at *3 fils*. This is one of Dubai's most famous, and famously understated, places to eat, serving Michelin-quality cuisine in humble, café-like surroundings and at bargain prices, with the focus on Japanese-style seafood, including produce flown direct from Tokyo's Tsukiji Market.

3.30PM

Balkan soul. Stretch your legs – and revive your appetite – with a brisk walk down the Jumeirah corniche with perhaps a break en route at the excellent Balkan-inspired *21 Grams* bistro, one of the city's best cafés. The coffee is excellent, and if you've room be sure to try a slice of the café's signature black sesame strudel, cherry phyllo pie or chocolate hazelnut baklava.

7.00PM

Zen cocktails. Head to the *Grosvenor House* hotel and start the evening with Asian-inspired cocktails at the spectacular *Buddha Bar*, one of Dubai's most visually impressive eating and drinking destinations.

8.30PM

Row at 45. Catch the lift up to the *Grosvenor House*'s 45th floor and strap yourself in for an evening of foodie heaven at Jason Atherton's *Row at 45* restaurant, one of the city's top fine-dining experiences. The seventeen-course tasting menu starts with amuse bouches in the champagne lounge, before proceeding to the main dining room and then finishing in the library over petit fours and teas.

Dubai for families

10.00AM

Have sand, will shovel. Begin your day on the extensive swathes of sand at the Dubai Marina Beach, perfect for splashing in the sea, building sandcastles or just lounging in the sun. There are also lots of watersports on offer including kid-friendly banana-boat and donut rides.

12AM

Take to the waves. Next, catch a boat for the 60-minute ride from the beach to the *Atlantis* resort at the tip of the Palm Jumeirah, an exhilarating ride across the waves offering superb views of coastal landmarks from the dramatic skyscrapers of the Marina to the giant fronds of the Palm Jumeirah artificial island.

1.00PM

Lunch on the Palm. After arriving at the *Atlantis* resort, grab some lunch at *Wavehouse*, a family-focused café overlooking the Surf's Up wave rider, with attached bowling alley and games arcade.

2.00PM

Under the sea. Explore the resort's wacky Lost Chambers: a stunning subterranean aquarium stuffed with shoals of colourful marine life swimming amongst the mysterious "ruins" of the lost city of Atlantis.

3.00PM

Jump into a sea of sharks. Grab your swimming kit and spend the rest of the afternoon exploring the state-of-the art Aquaventure waterpark, featuring master-blasters, water-coasters, speed slides, inner-tube rides and power-jets. Or test your nerve on the vertiginous Leap of Faith waterslide, which catapults you at stomach-churning speed down a transparent tunnel through a lagoon full of sharks.

6.00PM

One-track mind. Dry off then head back to the mainland aboard the dramatic Palm Monorail, a fun 15-minute ride on a driverless train running along a track high above the Palm, with great views over the island as the sun sets.

7.00PM

Evening in the souk. From the monorail, catch a cab north to the Madinat Jumeirah and grab an evening meal before spending some time exploring the quaint faux-Arabian alleyways and souvenir shops of the Souk Madinat Jumeirah and wandering the Madinat's idyllic waterfront, with magnificent views of the beautiful illuminated *Burj Al Arab* rising beyond.

History

Straddling trade routes between the ancient civilisations of southern Mesopotamia (present-day Iraq) and the Indus Valley, and later between Britain and India, the region covered by the modern United Arab Emirates (UAE) has welcomed, traded with and been influenced by foreign visitors for millennia.

FROM PREHISTORY TO ISLAM

The region now covered by the UAE and northern Oman was known as "Magan" to the ancient Sumerians as far back as 3000 BC. Evidence suggests that pearls were already being traded as early as the fifth millennium BC, while bones from the 3rd-millennium BC Bronze Age settlement of Umm an Nar near Abu Dhabi offer the world's earliest evidence of domesticated camels.

The region's population continued to grow during the Iron Age (1200–300 BC), by which time the area had been absorbed into the Persian Assyrian empire. Subsequent centuries saw the emergence of major urban centres at Mleiha, in Sharjah emirate, and at Ad-Dour, near Umm Al Qaiwain. Finds here include Greek pottery and Roman glass, while lettering on coins and inscriptions indicates that Aramaic, the language of Christ, was the lingua franca of the region during the pre-Islamic era. From the fourth century AD, a significant number of Persian Sassanids lived in the region, including many early Christians.

The rapid conversion of the Arabian Peninsula to Islam during the seventh century AD brought major changes as the first Islamic dynasty, the Ummayads, drove the Sassanids from the region, with Arabic replacing Aramaic and Islamic influences gradually permeating the area. The growing navigational skills of Arab seafarers – such as the famous Ibn Majid, from Ras al Khaimah emirate – also facilitated an expansion of trade, with ships travelling as far as East Africa, India and China, as revealed by discoveries of fine Chinese porcelain fragments at coastal sites.

THE MAKTOUM ERA

The earliest confirmed mention of the name "Dubai" is from 1580, when Venetian merchant Gasparo Balbi, attracted to the region by its pearls, referred in his writings to a place called "Dibei". The origins of the modern city appear to date back to the early eighteenth century, when a small settlement was established at the mouth of the Creek, developing gradually into a modest fishing and pearling town of under a thousand people, initially ruled by the sheikhs of Abu Dhabi.

In the nineteenth century, the British began consolidating their control of the trade route to India through a series of treaties, or "truces", with local rulers – hence the UAE's colonial name: The Trucial States. One such "truce" was signed in 1820 with

Sassanid- and Abbasid-era ruins at the Jumeirah Archaeological Site

Mohammed Bin Hazza, leader of Dubai – essentially the first formal recognition of Dubai as an entity separate from neighbouring Abu Dhabi and Sharjah.

Dubai's modern history really begins in 1833, however, with the arrival of Sheikh Maktoum bin Buti and around eight hundred of his followers, who had left their homes in Abu Dhabi in disgust at the repressive behaviour of the then ruler. Installed in Dubai, Sheikh Maktoum took over control of the town, inaugurating the Maktoum family dynasty which survives to this day.

The position of the Maktoums was initially precarious, wedged between the two far more powerful emirates of Abu Dhabi and Sharjah, although the signing of a further treaty with the British in 1835 afforded a measure of security. Pearling continued to be the mainstay of the town's economy, while sea trade also flourished, the souk expanded, and in 1841 the new settlement of Deira was established on the opposite side of the Creek. British influence continued to grow, resulting in further treaties including, most importantly, the 1892 Exclusive Agreement, whereby Dubai agreed to hand over all its foreign policy affairs to Britain in return for a guarantee of protection – an agreement which remained in force until Independence in 1971.

Another result of British influence was the arrival of the first Indian merchants, while hundreds of Iranian traders also started settling in the city from the 1890s onwards, attracted by offers of free land and zero taxation by the then ruler of Dubai, Sheikh Maktoum bin Hasher (r. 1894–1906). Iranian traders provided a huge boost to the city's economy and added a cosmopolitan twist to the local population, as well as introducing the wind-towers which are now one of the city's most distinctive sights.

NOTES

In Arabic names, "bin" and "Ibn" both mean "son of": Mohammed bin Rashid is Mohammed, son of Rashid. "Bint" means "daughter of".

SHEIKH RASHID

The village of Hatta dates back three thousand years

Dubai continued to flourish during the early twentieth century until the Great Depression in 1929 decimated the local pearling economy, while the discovery of a reliable method of producing cultured pearls soon afterwards wiped out what was left of the industry. Rising poverty ensued, and the Deira side of the Creek revolted against Maktoum rule, leading by 1939 to a state of virtual civil war within the city. The ruling family retained control only when the young Sheikh Rashid brutally crushed the rebellion (see page 35) and then faced down a further wave of popular protests inspired by the democratic Arab Nationalist movement led by Egyptian president Gamal Nasser.

Sheikh Rashid would go on to become one of Dubai's most visionary leaders, commonly referred to as the "Father of Modern Dubai". Finally succeeding his father Saeed in 1958, Rashid set about realising his vision for the future city. His first act was to dredge the Creek, a risky and enormously expensive project but one which, when finished in 1961, established Dubai as the best-equipped port in the region. Further developments followed: Dubai's first airport (opened 1960), the first bridge across the Creek (Maktoum Bridge, 1963) and, most importantly, the huge new Port Rashid (1971), which did more than anything else to drive modern Dubai's nascent economy. At the same time, as if to prove that fortune favours the brave, oil was discovered. Reserves were relatively modest compared to those in neighbouring Abu Dhabi, but the subsequent revenues provided much of the money needed to fund Dubai's major new infrastructure projects and launch it into the modern world.

INDEPENDENCE

Further challenges followed with Britain's announcement in 1968 that it intended to withdraw from the Gulf and grant independence to the various Trucial States, as they were still known. The region's rulers, who had been living comfortably under British protection since 1820, had no particular wish to see the end of Britain's military presence given the possible threat from much larger and more powerful neighbours in the shape of Iran and Saudi Arabia. Seeking safety in numbers, the emirates of Dubai, Abu Dhabi, Sharjah, Ajman, Fujairah and Umm al Qaiwain formed a new confederation known as the United Arab Emirates (a seventh emirate, Ras al Khaimah, joined soon afterwards). Many observers feared the new country would rapidly fall apart, although more than fifty years on it has proved more of a success than perhaps anyone could have hoped for at the time.

Dubai, meanwhile, continued to prosper within the new UAE. Business was booming and the population growing steadily, while further developments commissioned by the indefatigable Sheikh Rashid included the new World Trade Centre, Jebel Ali Port, the Shindagha Tunnel and the city's dry docks.

SHEIKH MOHAMMED

Sheikh Rashid suffered a stroke in 1982, and although he survived until 1990 the day-to-day running of the city increasingly fell to his four sons. The eldest, Sheikh Maktoum, was appointed official heir to the throne, although it was increasingly Rashid's third son, Mohammed, who provided the imagination and impetus driving further development. Mohammed continued to tread in his father's

The UAE's oldest mosque is at Badiyah, on the east coast

entrepreneurial footsteps, although focusing increasingly on service industries rather than infrastructure projects. His first major coup was the founding in 1985 of Emirates, now one of the world's most successful airlines, as well as creating numerous free-trade zones and specialised business enclaves, including Dubai Media City and Dubai Internet City, which encouraged large numbers of blue-chip global companies to set up their regional headquarters here.

As the new millennium dawned development went into overdrive, transforming the city almost beyond recognition and more than doubling its size. Leading landmarks included the soaring Emirates Tower (2000) and, most significantly, the stupendous *Burj Al Arab* (1999), whose iconic sail-shaped outline did more than anything else to establish Dubai in the global consciousness. Further spectacular mega-developments followed, including the

NAMING RIGHTS

As Dubai teetered on the edge of bankruptcy in 2008, rumour abounded as to what price the rulers of Abu Dhabi would extract in return for bailing out their profligate neighbour. In the end, Dubai wasn't obliged to relinquish any of its commercial crown jewels in return for the loan, although it did make one small but richly symbolic concession, renaming the vast new Burj Dubai skyscraper as the Burj Khalifa in honour of Abu Dhabi's ruler Sheikh Khalifa bin Zayed Al Nahyan – meaning that the name of a rival ruler now adorns the loftiest and most visible building in the city.

world's biggest shopping centre, Dubai Mall (2008) and tallest building, Burj Khalifa (2009). Meanwhile, entire new city districts were created almost from scratch around the Dubai Marina and in Downtown Dubai, not to mention the vast new Jumeirah Palm artificial island. Further increasingly lunatic mega-projects were announced on a seemingly weekly basis, most notably the vast Dubailand development (featuring the world's largest theme park and biggest hotel), along with other zany projects including the world's first five-star underwater hotel.

Then, in late 2008, just as it seemed the boom would never end, Dubai was brought crashing down to earth as the result of the global credit crunch. The real-estate market collapsed, investment fled, and Dubai, found itself suddenly teetering on the edge of bankruptcy. Abu Dhabi eventually came to the rescue with a massive bail-out package, although many of the city's mega-projects were cancelled or put on indefinite hold.

WAR IN YEMEN – AND A FAMILY AT WAR

Bankruptcy was thus averted, and although Dubai's prestige and financial standing took a significant hit, the city's recovery from the credit crunch was considerably faster than expected. Following years of steady recovery, 2015 also saw the opening of a new chapter in the brief history of the UAE when it joined the Saudi-led coalition battling Houthi forces in the ongoing civil war in Yemen – the country's first-ever military intervention abroad and a sign of the UAE's desire to project its growing economic and political power across the region. A number of Emirati troops were killed in early clashes, although these early losses paled into significance in early September 2015 when a Houthi missile caused an ammunition dump to explode, killing 52 Emirati troops in a single attack and sending shockwaves through the UAE.

A far more personal family scandal engulfed Dubai in early 2018 following the disappearance of Princess Latifa, one of Sheikh Mohammed's estimated thirty children. Attempting to flee Dubai, Latifa was approaching Goa in a private yacht before being intercepted just off the Indian coast – after which she vanished from public view.

Sheikh Mohammed, Vice President and Prime Minister of the UAE, as well as emir of Dubai

The case of the missing princess attracted widespread international attention, with growing fears for Latifa's safety and ongoing uncertainty concerning her whereabouts. Government sources, meanwhile, claimed that the princess had been suffering mental-health problems and was now being cared for by her family in Dubai.

Over the following months Latifa's friends received a series of messages in which the princess alleged that she was being held captive in a Jumeirah villa and suffering repeated physical and mental abuse. Ongoing concerns over the fate of the princess continued to simmer, with her case being escalated all the way up to the UN Human Right Office. Eventually, in May 2021 photos emerged of the princess sitting with friends in the Mall of the Emirates. The story thus fizzled out into a rather ambiguous conclusion and as of 2023 the princess was believed to be living a normal life in Paris, although details remain scant.

Further fissures within the Dubai ruling family emerged in February 2019 when Sheikh Mohammed unexpectedly divorced his second wife, Princess Haya, amidst claims that Haya had been

Construction of the Burj Khalifa, the world's tallest building

conducting an affair with her bodyguard. Haya subsequently left Dubai with two of her children, eventually taking up residence in the UK. Shortly afterwards Sheikh Mohammed began legal proceedings to have the two children returned to Dubai.

The case eventually made its way to the UK High Court who found, after lengthy legal proceedings, that "on the balance of probabilities" Sheikh Mohammed had orchestrated the forcible return of Latifa in 2018 (as well as the unlawful abduction of her sister Shamsa, who had also attempted to flee Dubai back in 2000). The court ruled in Haya's favour, ordering Sheikh Mohammed to pay a settlement of over £250m.

TO MARS AND BEYOND

Despite the huge damage to Sheikh Mohammed's once lustrous international reputation, Dubai continues to go from strength to strength. Proof of the city's increasing resilience was demonstrated by its handling of the Covid pandemic, from which it emerged with its economy largely intact (in stark contrast to 2008), and with a relatively low number of fatalities given the city's size and population density. Meanwhile, July 2020 saw the start of UAE Emirates Mars Mission with the launch of the "Hope" probe, while the country's growing regional and global political influence was acknowledged when it was appointed for a two-year term to the UN Security Council in 2021. Dubai's hosting of Expo 2020 and 2023 UN Climate Change Conference (COP 28) further gilded the city's status as a leading global destination – although the massive floods which bought the entire metropolis to a virtual standstill in April 2024 also gave notice of Dubai's vulnerability to the ongoing effects of global warming.

Tourism too continues to flourish, with Dubai regularly appearing in Top 5 lists of the world's leading city destinations, although this is now just one element in the city's highly diversified post-oil economy, with revenues from sectors such as finance, shipping, business and real estate also contributing significantly to Dubai's ever-increasing prosperity.

CHRONOLOGY

2700–2000 BC A Bronze Age settlement is established at Al Sufouh.
1st century BC An Iron Age village is established at Al Ghusais.
6th century AD The Sassanids set up a trading post in Jumeira.
AD 632 The region converts to Islam. Arabic replaces Aramaic.
1580 Earliest surviving reference to 'Dibei' by Gasparo Balbi of Venice.
1793 A dependency of Abu Dhabi, Dubai is a fishing and pearling village of 1,200 people located around the Creek.
1833 Maktoum Bin Buti Al Maktoum and 800 members of the Al Bu Falasah section of the Bani Yas tribe settle in Shindagha.

The Poland Pavilion at Expo 2020 in Dubai

1853 The Perpetual Treaty of Maritime Truce is signed by Britain and local sheikhs. The region becomes the Trucial Coast.
1902 Increased customs duties in the Persian port of Lingah prompt more foreign traders to migrate to Dubai's free-trade zone.
1912 Sheikh Saeed Bin Maktoum becomes ruler.
1958 Sheikh Rashid Bin Saeed, 'the Father of Dubai', becomes ruler.
1966 Oil is discovered in Dubai's offshore Fatah field.
1969 Oil production begins.
1971 The UAE becomes an independent federation on 2 December. Abu Dhabi's Sheikh Zayed Bin Sultan Al Nahyan becomes president, Sheikh Rashid of Dubai is appointed vice-president.
1980s First mall (Al Ghurair Centre, 1981), Dubai Duty Free (1983), Emirates airline (1985) and Jebel Ali Free Zone (1985) all established.
1990 Sheikh Maktoum Bin Rashid becomes ruler.
2006 Sheikh Maktoum dies. Sheikh Mohammed becomes ruler of Dubai.
2008 The world financial crisis hits Dubai.
2010 Opening of the Burj Khalifa, the world's tallest building.
2013 Population of Dubai reaches 2.1 million, up from 59,000 in 1967.
2014 Amnesty International reproaches UAE for an unparalleled clampdown on dissent since 2011, when a group of activists called for political reforms.
2015 UAE takes part in the Saudi Arabian airstrikes on the Houthis in Yemen.
2017 Five UAE diplomats are killed in Afghanistan bombings. UAE are accused of hacking Qatari government media sites.
2021 Dubai hosts the Expo 2020, delayed due to Covid-19.
2023 UAE hosts the United Nations Climate Change Conference (COP 28).
2024 In April, Dubai experiences devastating, record-breaking flash floods.

The Burj Khalifa dominates the city

Places

Dubai boasts an eclectic and ever-expanding array of sights. The old city districts of **Shindagha**, **Bur Dubai** and **Deira** are home to a marvellous collection of busy souks alongside time-warped wind-towered houses and cultural museums, while heading south the modern city boasts some of the planet's most eye-bending contemporary attractions, from the wacky skyscrapers of **Sheikh Zayed Road** through to the **Burj Khalifa** (the world's tallest building), the iconic **Burj Al Arab** hotel and the bristling high-rises of **Dubai Marina**. A long swathe of **beach** lining the coast provides plenty of space to relax, while a string of extravagantly themed **malls**, one of the world's largest artificial islands and the largest indoor ski slope provide other diversions along the way.

NOTES

Relations between the two Creekside districts of Bur Dubai and Deira have not always been harmonious. During the late 1930s, tensions rose across the city amid increasing poverty and worsening economic and living conditions. The **merchants' majlis**, established in 1938, rebelled against the authority of the Bur Dubai-based Sheikh Saeed and seized Deira, declaring independence. In 1939, Saeed's son, the young Sheikh Rashid, was permitted to arrive in Deira under a temporary truce but arrived with his Bedouin retainers and shot down many of the rebel leaders. The previous order was restored, and those who survived were blinded in one eye as punishment and forced to "buy" their remaining eye on payment of a sizeable sum.

SHINDAGHA

HIGHLIGHTS

- Heritage museums, see page 36
- Shindagha promenade, see page 39

Strung out along a curling promontory at the mouth of the Creek, the historic area of **Shindagha** has now been swallowed up by Bur Dubai but was once a completely distinct settlement, separated from the rest of Dubai by an arm of the Creek which flooded at high tide. This is most likely where the original fishing and pearling village of Dubai first developed: a modest cluster of simple *barasti* palm-frond shacks, plus a few mud-brick houses.

AL SHINDAGHA MUSEUM

Most of Shindagha has been lovingly preserved, with a long line of traditional low-rise, dun-coloured coral-stone buildings lined up along the Creek. Many of these have now been pressed into service as part of the vast new **Al Shindagha Museum** ❶ (www.

A reconstruction of a traditional dhow

WHERE TO SHOOT THE BEST PICTURES

Strong sunlight and spectacular sights makes Dubai great for photography, although light can be harsh in the middle of the day and a quality polarising filter is worth its weight in gold, while you'll need a tripod to capture the city's brilliant after-dark views.

The Creek is photogenic from just about everywhere. There a classic view looking inland from the south end of the Shindagha waterfront, with skyscrapers and minarets galore, or try some shots of abras departing the Bur Dubai abra station. Nearby **Al Fahidi** is another photographic dream – try shooting from the west side of the area with the slender white Diwan minaret in the background. Down in the modern city, the soaring **Burj Khalifa** is another essential subject. Head to the entrance of *The Palace* hotel for another iconic Dubai viewpoint. New buildings have now blocked the classic view of the **Burj Al Arab** from the north, so head to **Madinat Jumeirah**, which offers marvellous view of Dubai's most iconic landmark surreally framed between the faux-antique wind towers of the Madinat. Further afield, shots of the pink flamingos at the **Ras al Khor** sanctuary framed against the city's skyscrapers are another quintessential Dubai image, while keen wildlife photographers should visit the beautiful **Dubai Desert Conservation Reserve** for timeless desert imagery.

visitdubai.com/en/places-to-visit/al-shindagha-museum; charge), an ambitious attempt to chart every aspect of the city's history and culture in microscopic detail. The "museum" is actually spread out over around thirty different houses across the district, with individual buildings (or groups of buildings) devoted to particular themes ranging from traditional jewellery, perfume and poetry through to historical coverage of the city's origins and spectacular modern growth, plus some interesting sections dedicated to its seafaring, dhow-building and pearling past.

The historic highlight of the museum is undoubtedly **Al Maktoum House** ❷, former residence of the ruling Maktoum family, who lived

Peregrine falcons have a new role: hunting pigeons

here until the late 1950s (including the current ruler of Dubai, Sheikh Mohammed, whose early years were spent in the house amidst a crowd of servants, retainers, assorted domestic animals and perhaps the occasional camel). Located by the water, the house offered a strategic vantage point for former rulers of Dubai – including the pioneering Sheikh Saeed, grandfather of the present ruler, and his legendary son Sheikh Rashid, "the Father of Dubai" – to watch sea trade moving in and out of the Creek. Originally built in 1896 (although completely reconstructed since then), this is one of Shindagha's most impressive structures, built of coral stone, covered in lime and sand-coloured plaster and arranged around a spacious central courtyard with four *barjeel*, or wind-towers (an innovative early form of air conditioning introduced by traders from Iran) at the corners.

A few doors further along the Creek, the eye-catching **Sheikh Obaid Bin Thani House** of 1916 has also been incorporated into Al Shindagha Museum. The "Emerging City" displays inside are interesting, but it's the building itself which really impresses, particularly the beautiful courtyard with its flamboyantly cusped arches and intricately carved stone balustrades.

West of here, Shindagha assumes a more practical tone, dominated by **Port Rashid**. Construction on this deep-water harbour began in 1967, instigated by Sheikh Rashid during an era of massive public works funded by the emirate's new oil revenues and designed to provide it with a diversified modern industrial and commercial base. This is where you'll find the modern **Dubai Cruise Terminal**, while the port also provides an unlikely home for the historic British *QE2* ocean liner, now permanently moored here and repurposed as an atmospherically time-warped floating hotel.

CREEKSIDE PROMENADE

One of the Shindagha's most attractive features is undoubtedly its breezy **Creekside promenade**, which runs from the tip of the peninsula all the way back through Bur Dubai and beyond, offering marvellous views up and down the Creek and over the water

BREEDING FALCONS

The fastest creature on the planet has been used by falconers for hunting for thousands of years, although nowadays the ancient skill of falconry is maintained for sport rather than survival. Before weapons, peregrine falcons – which can achieve speeds of 320kph (200mph) in a dive – were used by *bedu* hunters to catch food. Wild falcons were caught and trained in two or three weeks at the start of the hunting season in October. Favoured prey was the houbara bustard, a desert bird the size of a heron, whose meat could be vital to a family's survival. At the end of the season, in March, the falcon would be freed.

Today, falcons are no longer captured, but reared from hatchlings. Possession of a prized falcon is a major status symbol amongst the city's Emirati elite, with some birds selling for US$50,000 or more – literally worth their weight in gold, or perhaps slightly more. Falcons are also put to practical use and employed to scare away flocks of pigeons from many of the city's more prestigious high-rises, keeping properties clear of unsightly bird droppings – one of the reasons the *Burj Al Arab* still looks so beautifully white after all these years.

A water taxi on the Creek, with the Juma Grand Mosque beyond

to Deira's tangle of traditional bazaars and modernist high-rises. Following the waterfront inland from Shindagha takes you past the busy *abra* station and then on through the Textile Souk. Past here you'll reach the Juma Grand Mosque, with its impressive 70m- (231ft-) high minaret, and the Emiri Diwan (or Ruler's Court), beyond which the waterfront walk can be extended for a further kilometre through the attractive new Al Seef development. With buildings crowded in on either side of the waterway, *abras* loaded with passengers criss-crossing the Creek and colourful dhows laden with exports for Pakistan, India or East Africa sailing serenely by, the scene is reminiscent of a Canaletto painting, recalling an old nickname for Dubai you don't often hear these days: "Venice of the Middle East".

BUR DUBAI

HIGHLIGHTS

- Al Fahidi Fort, see page 41
- Al Fahidi Historical Neighbourhood, see page 42
- Al Seef, see page 44
- Bur Dubai Souk, see page 44

If Shindagha was the residential heart of old Dubai, then **Bur Dubai** was undoubtedly its central business district and commercial hub, home to a multicultural mix of Iranian and Indian merchants who settled here with their families from 1894, when Sheikh Maktoum Bin Hasher declared free-trade status for the city. The lasting influence of these immigrants can still be seen in the spiky wind-towered houses dotting the time-warped Al Fahidi Historical Neighbourhood.

AL FAHIDI FORT

Dubai's oldest surviving building, **Al Fahidi Fort** ❸ was built between 1787 and 1799 to guard the landward approach to the town. The Portuguese-influenced fortress formerly served as the

PEARL DIVING

In the centuries before oil was discovered, pearling was the mainstay of the Dubai economy, involving the majority of the settlement's men. From June to September, crews of between fifteen and sixty stayed at sea for up to four months, moving from one pearl oyster bed to another and sheltering from storms on Gulf islets. Equipped with little more than a nose clip, ear plugs and finger pads, and surviving on a diet of fish and rationed water, the men would dive on weighted ropes to depths of around 15m (49ft) up to fifty times a day. In two to three minutes under water they could collect up to a dozen pearl oysters.

Pearls were graded according to their size, colour and shape. In the early twentieth century, the best pearls or *jiwan* (a derivative of "Grade One" or "G-One") could fetch 1,500 rupees, although while Dubai's pearl merchants grew wealthy, a diver's wages for the entire season could be as little as 30 rupees. Famous for their rose colouring, Dubai pearls were traded in India, from where they were sent to Paris. The introduction of Japanese cultured pearls from the 1930s onwards devastated the Gulf industry virtually overnight, however, and after struggling on for another decade, the last great pearling expedition sailed from Dubai in 1949.

ruler's residence and the seat of government, as well as providing a refuge for the town's inhabitants in the event of attack. The building itself – a simple, square, high-walled compound with corner towers covered in sun-baked plaster – is an arresting sight among the modern apartment blocks and office buildings of Al Fahidi Street, while a fine wooden pearling *dhow* stands on the plaza in front. The fort formerly housed the excellent **Dubai Museum**, although it has been closed for years now, with no reopening date in sight.

Between the fort and the Creek is the landmark **Juma Grand Mosque**, one of the oldest in Dubai, originally built in 1900 (although completely reconstructed in 1998). The impressively large building boasts the tallest minaret in the city, plus nine large domes, 45 small domes and space for 1,200 worshippers. Free guided tours (Thurs–Sun mornings; www.islamicic.com/mosque) offer non-Muslims the chance to have a look at the serene interior.

AL FAHIDI HISTORICAL NEIGHBOURHOOD

East of Al Fahidi Fort, a dense cluster of picturesque old wind towers announces the presence of **Al Fahidi Historical Neighbourhood** ❹, one of the city's most absorbing neighbourhoods. The area was originally settled by expat traders from Bastak and Lingah (hence the area's original name, Bastakiya, which is still often used today) on the coast of modern-day Iran. The first traders were attracted to Dubai from the late 1890s onwards thanks to a series of tax breaks and other incentives, and the area remained a flourishing epicentre of local commerce through until the 1970s, when the descendants of the original merchants decamped to more modern accommodation elsewhere. By the mid-1990s most of the old buildings were on the verge of collapse and were saved from demolition only at the last moment, after which the entire district was lovingly restored to its present condition.

Modern Al Fahidi is pleasantly somnolent (except during the busy SIKKA Art Fair, held here in March), with a cluster of tall,

The old merchant quarter of Al Fahidi

almost windowless traditional buildings arranged around a disorienting tangle of alleyways, built deliberately narrow to provide shade during the heat of the day. Topping almost every building are the quarter's famous wind-towers, rising to heights of up to 15m (49ft) and providing an ingenious early form of air-conditioning by channelling breezes into the rooms below. The walls of each house, meanwhile, were made of coral stone, which, thanks to its porous nature, has low thermal conductivity, keeping temperatures inside to a minimum. Ground-floor windows were largely eschewed on the grounds of privacy and security.

Many of the old buildings have now been repurposed as miniature museums (all free) highlighting different aspects traditional life. Easily the best is the engaging **Coffee Museum** (www.coffeemuseum.ae), while others include the Arabic Calligraphy Museum, Coins Museum,

Philately House and Architectural Heritage Department. Exhibits are low-key, although it's worth ducking inside at least a couple for the chance to look at the beautifully restored interiors.

Further memorable examples of Al Fahidi's historic houses include the venerable **Majlis** and **XVA galleries** (see page 95) – the latter has a gorgeous courtyard café, while nearby you'll also find the **Sheikh Mohammed Centre For Cultural Understanding** (see page 140), which organises excellent walking tours of the quarter.

AL SEEF

West of Al Fahidi, the peaceful **Al Seef** district meanders alongside the Creekside waterfront for over a kilometre. The area's canopied alleyways, quaint squares and wind-towered traditional houses look as old as anything in the city but are in fact entirely modern, the entire "historic" district having been dreamt up by property developers Meraas and opened in 2017. It's not exactly authentic, but makes an attractive place for idle wandering, pedestrianized throughout and with dozens of small shops and cafés to explore, as well as the entertaining **Museum of Illusions** (www.museumofillusions.ae; charge), home to a diverting array of brain-twisting exhibits.

Walking south along the waterfront, the views are increasingly dominated by a cluster of modernist structure rising above the Creek on the opposite side of the water in Deira. These include the anvil-shaped *Sheraton Dubai Creek Hotel & Towers*, the minimalist Dubai Chamber of Commerce and, most impressively Carlos Ott's 125m (410ft) **National Bank of Dubai Building** ❺ whose dramatic, sail-shaped glass facade serves as a kind of gigantic mirror, reflecting boats on the Creek below during the day and the dazzling rays of the setting sun towards dusk.

BUR DUBAI SOUK

Running alongside the Creek west of Al Fahidi Fort, **Bur Dubai Souk** ❻ (also known as the Textile Souk, the Old Souk and the Grand

Souk Bur Dubai) is the oldest and still one of the busiest in the city, crowded most days with throngs of wandering tourists browsing the souk's touristy array of souvenirs and colourful fabrics. The tiny shops lining the souk have been neatly restored, with heavy wooden doors and dun-coloured plastered exteriors, while an impressive traditional wooden roof overhead provides welcome shade.

Near the main entrance to the souk look out for the **Bait al Wakeel**, the city's first office building when it opened in 1935. Originally occupied by the British Gray Mackenzie shipping company it now houses the pleasant *Bait Al Wakeel* restaurant, with fine Creek views.

A few steps down the road from the main entrance to the souk, **Bur Dubai Abra Station** is a fascinating spot to stand and watch the traffic on the Creek. For one dirham you can catch an *abra* from here for the five-minute ride over the waters to Al Sabkha Abra Station in Deira, offering marvellous views of the dense tangle of traditional buildings, skyscrapers, minarets and wind-towers lining both sides of the Creek. A second abra route runs across the Creek from the smaller **Bur Dubai Old Souk Station** tucked away in the middle of the Bur Dubai souk.

South of the souk itself, bustling **Al Fahidi Road** is lined with shops stacked high with mobile phones

Jewellery at the Gold Souk

and shiny watches, as well as colourful textile emporia, their windows stuffed with a colourful array of Indian clothing and fabrics. Further south, Bur Dubai's main thoroughfare, **Khalid Bin al Waleed Road**, is home to a plethora of computer shops as well as the cavernous **BurJuman** (www.burjuman.com), the old city's largest and fanciest mall.

DEIRA

HIGHLIGHTS

The district of **Deira**, on the north side of the Creek, was first settled in 1841 when an outbreak of smallpox prompted many of the inhabitants of Bur Dubai to cross the water and construct new houses. The new settlement swiftly prospered, with the main market, Al Souk al Kabeer, becoming the largest in the region during the second half of the nineteenth century. By 1908 there were 1,600 houses and 350 shops in Deira compared to just 200 and 50 respectively in Bur Dubai, and even now the area feels noticeably busier and more built up than the old city south of the Creek.

THE GOLD SOUK

At the heart of Deira, Dubai's famous **Gold Souk** ❼ is the old city's most popular attraction: a single street, shaded by a high wooden roof and lined with dozens of small shops piled high with a dazzling array of jewellery, ranging from minimalist European-style designs to large and fantastically ornate Arabian-style necklaces, bangles and ear-rings.

One of the world's largest centres for the trade of gold bullion, Dubai has been trading in the precious metal for well over a hundred years – indeed it was gold that saw Dubai through one of its leanest periods when the bottom fell out of the local pearl market in the 1930s. Historically it was demand from India that drove trade, and even today it's the softer, higher-carat golds favoured on the subcontinent that predominate in the souk's window displays. Gold prices here remain amongst the lowest in the world, although haggling is essential (and expected) if you do decide to buy.

A fabric salesman in Deira

THE SPICE SOUK

Squeezed in between the Gold Souk and the Creek, Dubai's **Spice Souk** ❽ (signed as the "Herbs Market") is one of the smallest but prettiest in the old city, featuring a pair of narrow lanes lined with a couple of dozen shops with huge sacks of spices piled up in front (or just follow the scent of spices perfuming the air – you might well smell the souk before you see it). Goods on sale range from relatively workaday ingredients – cloves, cardamom, cinnamon – through to more exotic local products such as rose petals (used as an infusion to add a delicate flavour to drinks) and frankincense – the latter in particular makes an unusual and extremely fragrant souvenir.

Sprawling around the back of the Spice Souk, the indeterminate **Grand Souk Deira** is a lot larger but relatively humdrum. The whole place has been extensively renovated over recent years and is now popular with some of the city's pushiest touts, although the merchandise on offer – mainly workaday household items and assorted toys – is uninspiring.

The souk is also home to the tiny but atmospheric **Museum of the Poet Al Oqaili** (http://bit.ly/Oqaili), hidden away around the back in the former house of noted poet Mubarak bin Hamad al Manea al Oqaili (1875–1954). The exhibits are decidedly dull, but

Spices, nuts and seeds on sale at the Spice Souk

the house itself is well worth a look, with two storeys set around a shady central courtyard, embellished with delicately carved stone windows and wooden balustrades.

Tucked away on Old Baladiya Road around the back of the Gold Souk, **Al Ahmadiya School** ❾ and the **Heritage House** were formerly two of old Dubai's most engaging sights. The former was once the oldest school – and one of the prettiest buildings – in the city, while the latter gave a good sense of how life in old-time Dubai really looked. Unfortunately both have been closed for renovations for a number of years now, with no scheduled reopening date in sight, but are well worth a visit in the event that they open their doors to the public again.

EAST OF THE GOLD SOUK

Exiting the Gold Souk via the main entrance and heading east along Sikkat al Khail Road brings you immediately to the so-called **Perfume Souk,** comprising a line of shops along Sikkat al Khail and Al Soor streets selling a mix of Western brands (not necessarily genuine) and more flowery local scents. Most places can also mix up a bespoke perfumes for you from the rows of glass scent bottles lined up behind the counters.

Continuing west of the Gold and Perfume souks, Deira continues in a sprawl of souks stretching for the best part of a kilometre before reaching Al Musallah Street. The first section, loosely known as **Al Sabkha Souk**, comprises a rather indeterminate area of small shops arranged around the maze of narrow, pedestrianized alleyways which run south from Sikkat al Khail Road down towards the Creek. Most of the shops here are Indian-run, selling colourful, low-grade cloth for women's clothes, along with large quantities of mass-produced plastic toys and cheap household goods. It's all rather down-at-heel, but makes for an interesting stroll, especially in the area at the back of the Al Sabkha bus station, the densest and busiest part of the bazaar.

MUNICIPALITY MUSEUM

Located on the edge of the Spice Souk, opposite the Deira Old Souk Abra Station, the modest little **Municipality Museum** occupies the quaint old balconied building which originally housed the city's first municipal offices from 1958 to 1964 – the 1950s municipality had just six employees compared to over twenty thousand today. Exhibits include assorted charts, municipal stamps and other documents including the 1966 decree ordering traffic to drive on the right (vehicles had previously driven, British-style, on the left) and the groundbreaking city plan of 1960 showing the proposed development of Deira and Bur Dubai – extremely small beer compared to more recent developments, but impressively ambitious for its time.

DEIRA CREEKSIDE

Stretching along the Creek close to the Spice Souk, the ***dhow* wharfage** ❿ is one of the old city's highlights, with dozens of marvellous old wooden dhows moored along the waterfront and great piles of cargo – tyres, spare car parts, electrical goods – stacked up beside, while porters scamper around busily loading and unloading their vessels. Despite their antiquated appearance, dhows still play an important role in the economy of modern Dubai, transporting cargoes between Dubai and neighbouring emirates, or occasionally as far afield as India, Pakistan and East Africa, and bringing goods directly into the heart of the city via the Creek – a route inaccessible to larger ships (which dock at the city's modern container ports at Port Rashid and Jebel Ali).

There's a second dhow wharfage around 1km along the Creekside, occupying a trio of purpose-built quays in the shadow of the Carlos Ott's **National Bank of Dubai** building (see page 44).

Inland from here it's a short walk to the **Clocktower Roundabout**, at the junction of Maktoum Bridge and Al Maktoum Road. Built in 1962, the clocktower is one of Dubai's oldest landmarks and one of the few structures to have survived five decades

Old dhows lining Deira Creekside

of development – a rare visual reference point in the changing face of the city. Overlooking Clocktower Roundabout, the identical towers of the **Marriott Executive Apartments Complex** are connected by a distinctive 74m (242ft) skybridge.

WEST OF THE CENTRE

Further down Baniyas Road near the international airport, the suburb of **Garhoud** boasts a varied range of attractions. Most people visit to shop at **Deira City Centre** (www.citycentredeira.com), one of Dubai's oldest mega-malls, and still popular despite having long since been eclipsed by newer and more glamorous shopping destinations across the city.

Past here stretch the beautifully manicured grounds of the **Dubai Creek Golf Club** (www.dubaigolf.com), best known for

NOTES

Dubai Creek was a landing area for Imperial Airways' flying boats in the late 1930s and 1940s.

its landmark **clubhouse** ⓫ inspired by the shape of the traditional *dhow* sail, with three "sails" entwined to create a tent-like structure – like a miniature Dubai remake of the Sydney Opera House. The adjacent **Dubai Yacht Club** is home to a lively cluster of restaurants, while stretching beyond is the idyllic **Park Hyatt** hotel, with its long sequence of white, Moorish-style buildings topped with cute blue domes spread out along the Creek.

Facing the *Park Hyatt* on the opposite side of the Creek, the spacious **Creekside Park** ⓬ runs for over 3km (2 miles) alongside the Creek between Maktoum and Garhoud bridges, providing a welcome expanse of greenery close to the city centre. It's also home to the vividly coloured buildings of **Children's City** (www.childrencity.ae; charge), a fun, interactive learning attraction for kids aged from two to fifteen.

WAFI

Not far from Creekside Park, the quirky **Wafi Mall** ⓭ (www.wafi.com) looks like a little slice of Las Vegas dropped into the middle of the Dubai, with an Egyptian-themed design featuring a zany mishmash of huge pharaonic statues, hieroglyphs, and half a dozen miniature pyramids dotted across the sprawling rooflines. It's kitsch but entertaining, while the complex also provides one of the city's most attractive shopping and eating destinations.

Wafi is also where you'll find the futuristic new **AYA** (www.aya-universe.com; charge) attraction – a kind of immersive visual extravaganza for the Instagram age. Inside, the twelve elaborately mirrored, sense-twisting spaces are filled with swirling visual effects which cover every available surface – submarine corals, kaleidoscopic fractals, exploding galaxies. Endlessly refracted images create the illusion of vast plains covered in luminous flowers or endless starry skies, while solid floors transform into whorls of light and drops of water fall upwards. Just be careful not to walk into any walls.

Attached to Wafi, the similarly kitsch but undeniably pretty **Khan Murjan Souk** is one of Dubai's finest exercises in Orientalist chic, with virtually every available surface covered in lavishly detailed Arabian-style design, featuring elaborate Moroccan-style tilework, intricately carved wooden doors and ceilings, and huge hanging lamps, plus over a hundred shops retailing all manner of upmarket Arabian (and other) handicrafts.

Next door to Wafi – and continuing the Egyptian theme – the vast postmodern pyramid of the **Raffles Hotel** provides the area with its most dramatic landmark, visible for miles around and particularly impressive after dusk, when the glass-walled summit of the pyramid is lit up from within, glowing magically in the darkness. Inside, the main foyer is well worth a look, with huge Egyptian-style columns covered in colourful hieroglyphs. On the opposite side of Wafi, the soaring new **Sofitel Obelisk** is another postmodern Egyptian-inspired landmark – duck into the reception area for a glimpse of the hotel's gloriously over-the-top pharaonic decor.

The Dubai Creek Golf and Yacht Club

NOTES

The name given to wooden boats in the Arabian Gulf is *dhow*, from the Swahili word for boat, *dau*. These traditional cargo and fishing vessels are still a common sight on Dubai Creek.

KARAMA

Immediately south of Bur Dubai, the low-rent, nondescript 1970s suburb of **Karama** is home to some of the legions of Indian, Pakistani and Filipino expatriate workers – waitresses, taxi drivers, builders and shopkeepers – who supply so much of the city's labour. It's a great place to sample some of the city's ethnic cuisines, with dozens of often excellent (and always inexpensive) Indian and Pakistani cafés which have earned Karama the nickname "curry corridor". The district is also famous for its thriving trade in fake-designer gear and other cheap and cheerful stuff – you won't get more than a few paces into the main **Karama Souk** ⓮ before being regaled with offers of "cheap copy watch" and the like. The quality of many of the fakes is surprisingly high, although prices can be unexpectedly steep – if you do decide to buy, check workmanship carefully and bargain like mad.

Immediately north of the souk, diminutive **Karama Park is** the social heart of the suburb, usually busy after dark with half a dozen games of cricket and crowds of strolling expat Indians, Pakistanis and Filipinas wandering beneath the trees.

On the south side of Karama, the wonderfully weird **Dubai Frame** ⓯ (www.dubaiframe.ae; charge) can be regarded either as a spectacularly large picture frame or a very oddly shaped building – the brainchild of Mexican architect Fernando Donis, who stated that Dubai had enough landmarks and already and that rather than adding another he would create a frame large enough to capture the entire city. Standing over 150m, an elevator carries visitors to the observation platform at the top of the structure, offering peerless views of both old and new cities, while a museum at the base showcases Dubai's history and hints at future developments

– don't miss the fun film at the end of the tour showing a fantastically futuristic vision of Dubai as it might look in the year 2200. Note that limited access to the viewing deck means you'll likely have to queue for the best part of an hour to get in, and probably even longer at weekends.

SHEIKH ZAYED ROAD

HIGHLIGHTS

- South along Sheikh Zayed Road, see page 57
- Downtown Dubai and the Burj Khalifa, see page 59
- Around Downtown Dubai, see page 60
- City Walk and Business Bay, see page 64

The impressive entrance to the Egyptian-themed Wafi Mall

South of Karama, Dubai changes character dramatically as the neck-cricking towers of Sheikh Zayed Road rear into view, signalling the beginnings of the modern city and its ever-expanding array of super-sized skyscrapers, malls, artificial islands and other mega-developments which now march down the coast all the way to Dubai Marina, 25km to the south.

The northernmost section of **Sheikh Zayed Road** itself, between the World Trade Centre and Dubai Mall, is the most dramatic thoroughfare in the city, with a huge ten-lane highway running between a long line of slender skyscrapers in a range of postmodern styles ranging from the sleekly futuristic to the entertainingly daft.

Guarding the northern end of the strip, the **Dubai World Trade Centre** building was the tallest building in the Middle East when it opened in 1979. Commissioned by the visionary Sheikh Rashid, this 39-storey edifice was widely regarded as a massive white elephant when it was first built, standing as it did in the middle of what was then empty desert far from the old city centre. In fact, history has entirely vindicated Rashid's daring gamble. The tower proved an enormous success with foreign companies and US diplomats, who established a consulate here and used it as a major base for monitoring affairs in nearby Iran. The centre also served as an important anchor for future development along the strip, and it's a measure of Sheikh Rashid's far-sighted ambition that his alleged *folie de grandeur* has long since been overtaken by much larger and more glamorous structures further down the road.

Just south of the Trade Centre rise the iconic **Emirates Towers** ⓰, completed in 2000 and comprising a 355m- (1,163ft-) high office tower – at one point the tallest building in the Middle East and Europe – and the 309m- (1,014ft-) high *Jumeirah Emirates Towers Hotel*. Designed by Hong Kong architect Hazel Wong, the two slender triangular towers are clad in silver aluminium with copper and silver reflective glass, creating (as Wong describes it) "a *pas de deux* in which the building facades capture the changing

Museum of the Future

light of the desert sun and show off the dramatic integrated illumination at nightfall". It's worth popping into the entrance of the hotel tower for a glimpse of the stunning thirty-storey atrium, with pod-shaped glass elevators slithering up and down the walls.

SOUTH ALONG SHEIKH ZAYED ROAD

Facing the Emirates Towers, the wacky new **Museum of the Future** ⓱ (www.museumofthefuture.ae/en; charge) has already established itself as one of Dubai's most brilliantly original and instantly recognisable landmarks. Opened on the symbolically palindromic date of February 22, 2022, the gleaming ovoid structure has been described variously as either a giant eye or a squashed doughnut (or, more technically, as a "torus with an elliptical void"), while the elaborate swirls of Arabian calligraphy (they're actually windows) which cover

Burj Khalifa

the exterior simultaneously reference the region's cultural roots. Inside, hi-tech interactive displays evoke the world as it might become by the year 2071, with exhibits ranging from a digitally simulated rainforest through to a trip aboard the imaginary space station *OSS Hope*.

Tucked away behind the skyscrapers immediately south of the Emirates Towers, is Dubai's financial district, the **Dubai International Financial Centre (DIFC)** ⓲. Entrance to the complex is via The Gate building, a striking office block designed in the shape of an enormous postmodern archway. Past here, on the east side of the centre, the **Gate Village** is home to one of the city's best collections of art galleries (see page 95) plus a couple of excellent restaurants.

Back on Sheikh Zayed Road just south of the Emirates Towers, the thoroughly daft **Al Yaqoub Tower** is quite the strangest building along the strip: effectively a postmodern replica of London's Big Ben, minus the clock, although at 330m it's well over three times the height of the 96m-tall UK landmark. From here, it's an interesting twenty minute walk south along the road to the Dubai Mall past a string of skyscrapers. Notable landmarks along the way include the slender *Gevora Hotel*, officially the world's tallest hotel at a neck-cricking 356m, while just two doors down is the graceful *Rose Rayhaan* hotel (333m), which itself held the record from 2007 to 2012. Diagonally opposite is the soaring **Staybridge Suites** (formerly the Chelsea Tower), topped by what looks like an enormous toothpick, while slightly further south the needle-thin **AA Tower** echoes the shape of the *Gevora*, with a similar lattice-like spire at its summit. Past here is the imposing, Art Deco-influenced **Shangri-La Hotel** before the strip reaches a suitably odd end with the iconic Dusit Thani hotel, a towering glass-and-metal edifice inspired by the traditional Thai *wai*, a prayer-like gesture of welcome, although it looks more like a huge upended tuning fork thrust into the ground.

DOWNTOWN DUBAI AND THE BURJ KHALIFA

Immediately south of the Dusit Thani, Sheikh Zayed Road meets Financial Centre Road at the vast Interchange No. 1.Stretching away on the southern side of the junction, the massive **Downtown Dubai** development is home to several of the city's record-breaking modern landmarks, most notably the staggering **Burj Khalifa** ⓳, the world's tallest building, rising like an enormous needle out of the heart of the development. Opened in early 2010, the tower, at 828m (2,716ft) obliterated all previous records for the world's tallest man-made structure, smashing the previous record for the world's tallest building formerly held by Taipei 101 in Taiwan, at 509m (1,670ft) by a staggering 300m (984ft). The tower has also accumulated a host of other superlatives en route, including the building with the most floors (160), the world's highest and fastest elevators, plus the world's highest mosque (158th floor) and highest swimming pool (76th floor). Much of the tower is occupied by private apartments, while fifteen of the lower floors are home to the world's first *Armani Hotel*.

The astonishing size of the Burj Khalifa and its distinctively tapering outline is hard to grasp close up – the whole thing is best appreciated from a distance, from where you can properly appreciate the tower's jaw-dropping size, and the degree to which it dwarfs the surrounding high-rises, many of which are considerable structures in their own right. The simple but elegant design (by Adrian Smith of the Chicago architectural firm Skidmore, Owings and Merrill) is based on an unusual Y-shaped ground plan, with the three projecting wings being gradually stepped back as the tower rises, so that the entire building becomes progressively narrower as it gains height.

The easiest way to visit the tower is to take the expensive trip up to the misleadingly named "At the Top" observation deck (on floor 124, although there are actually 160 floors). Alternatively, the even pricier "At the Top Sky Experience" gets you up to level 148. Tours (www.burjkhalifa.ae; charge) leave from the ticket counter in the lower-ground floor of the Dubai Mall. Book as far in advance as possible, since reserved places can sell out weeks in advance and buying a ticket on the spot comes with a hefty surcharge (while visits to level 148 are only possible with a prior reservation).

AROUND DOWNTOWN DUBAI

Standing in the shadow of the world's tallest building, the spectacular **Dubai Fountain** ⓴ is, appropriately enough, the world's largest fountain: 275m (900ft) long, illuminated with over six thousand lights and with water-canons capable of firing plumes of water up to 150m (490ft) high. The fountain springs into action after dark, shooting choreographed jets of water into the air which "dance" in time to a range of Arabic, Hindi and classical songs, while multicoloured lights play to-and-fro across the watery plumes. "Performances" are staged every thirty minutes during the evening from 6pm and shows can be watched for free from anywhere around the lake. Short (25min) daytime abra rides around the fountain are also available, leaving from outside lake-facing entrance to the Dubai Mall.

Immediately beyond the fountain and lake lies yet another record-breaker, the gargantuan **Dubai Mall** ㉑ (www.thedubaimall.com), covering a total area of 12 million sq ft (1 million sq metres), with over 1200 shops spread across four floors, making it easily the world's largest mall measured by total area (although other malls contain more retail space). Flagship outlets include branches of the famous Galleries Lafayette and Bloomingdale's department stores, a huge branch of the Japanese bookseller Kinokuniya and an offshoot of London's famous Hamley's toy store. There is also a vast selection of upmarket designer stores, mainly concentrated along "Fashion Avenue", complete with its own catwalk, and in the ultra-cool boutiques of the ground-floor **Level Shoe District**, one of the most gorgeous pieces of retail interior design you'll ever see, plus an attractive Arabian-themed "souk" area. The latter also provides an incongruous home for the "**Dubai Dino**", a beautifully preserved, 7.6m-high skeleton of a 150-million-year-old *Diplodocus longus*, unearthed in Wyoming in 2008.

The mall is also home to the **Dubai Aquarium and Underwater Zoo** (www.thedubaiaquarium.com; charge). The aquarium's most

View of Dubai Fountain from Burj Khalifa

notable feature is the spectacular "viewing panel", towering over the shops by the Finance Centre Road entrance to the mall: a huge, floor-to-ceiling transparent acrylic panel filled with an extraordinary array of marine life, ranging from sand-tiger sharks and stingrays to colourful shoals of tiny tropical fish, all of which can be seen for free from the mall. Inside, the Underwater Zoo is more likely to appeal to children than adults, with displays themed after various different types of marine habitat and featuring an array of wildlife ranging from tiny cichlids and poison-dart frogs through to otters, penguins and seals.

Shops apart, the mall also boasts a host of other leisure attractions including some 120 cafés and restaurants, divided between various interior food courts and the bustling waterside terrace at the back of the mall overlooking the Dubai Fountain. Children will enjoy the off-beat KidZania "edu-tainment" attraction, while there's also an Olympic-size ice rink if you want to cool off in the heat of the day.

Heading back to the lake at the back of the mall, a small footbridge leads across to the "Old Town" development: a large swathe of low-rise, sand-coloured buildings with traditional Moorish styling. On the far side of the footbridge lies the cute little **Souk al Bahar** (Souk of the Sailor; www.soukalbahar.ae), a small, Arabian-themed mall specializing in traditional handicrafts and independent fashion. Further restaurants line the waterfront terrace outside, offering peerless views of the Burj Khalifa and Dubai Fountain after dark.

On the far side of the Souk al Bahar stands *The Palace* hotel, its sumptuous Moorish-style facade and richly decorated interior offering a surreal contrast to the futuristic Burj Khalifa rising directly behind.

Circling the entire downtown area, **Sheikh Mohammed bin Rashid Boulevard** is home to a growing number of restaurants and cafés and is also where you'll find Downtown Dubai's newest landmark, the **Dubai Opera House** (www.dubaiopera.com), opened in 2016 and designed by acclaimed Iraqi architect Zaha Hadid, whose dhow-shaped outline pays homage to traditional Arabian sailing vessels.

Further memorable views of the futuristic Downtown Dubai skyline can be had at **Sky Views Dubai** (www.skyviewsdubai.com; charge), occupying the 220m-high skybridge connecting the two towers of *The Address Sky View* hotel on the south side of the Dubai Mall. You get a very different perspective of the area here, being much lower than at the Burj Khalifa (a fact reflected in the ticket prices), but it's still a hugely impressive sight – and of course you can also see the Burj itself, since you're not on it. The see-through glass floor adds to the fun – if in doubt, don't look down. Tickets include a go on the small and gimmicky "Sky View Slide", arguably Dubai's most tragically underwhelming visitor experience. For more genuine thrills sign up for the **Edge Walk**, during which you'll be clipped onto the outside of the building and then led on a walk around an open platform at the top of the tower with nothing between you and the vertiginous drop below – you can even try swinging out over the parapet into mid-air if you've serious nerves of steel.

Nighttime traffic and illuminated skyscrapers on Mohammed bin Rashid Boulevard

CITY WALK AND BUSINESS BAY

Around 500m west of Sheikh Zayed Road, the new **City Walk** ㉒ (www.citywalk.ae/en) development offers a refreshing change of pace and scenery compared to the manic crowds of the Dubai Mall. Pedestrianized throughout, the spacious outdoor complex is one of the city's most enjoyable and laid-back places for idle shopping, supping and wandering, featuring a beautifully designed and relatively low-rise spread of suave modern buildings arranged around a series of spacious plazas and home to a good array of shops and restaurants, as well as the striking **Coca-Cola Arena**, hosting regular music and other events.

On the north side of the development, the enjoyable **Green Planet** "indoor zoo" (www.thegreenplanetdubai.com; charge) serves up another of Dubai's many faintly surreal experiences, offering the chance to explore a swathe of tropical rainforest in the heart of downtown. Enclosed within a striking "bio-dome" (actually more like a large glass cylinder), the artificial rainforest is home to over three thousand plant, animal and bird species including sloths, armadillos, flying foxes, anacondas, toucans and bats, centred on an ersatz waterfall and what's claimed to be the world's largest artificial tree.

Directly south of Downtown Dubai, the shiny **Business Bay** development comprises a further dense cluster of high-rises arranged around the Dubal Water Canal, which can also be explored from here either on foot or by bike or boat (see page 69). As the name suggests the area is aimed at corporate rather than tourist types, although there are a few local landmarks worth a quick look.

Exiting the metro and heading right at the first main intersection brings you to the **JW Marriott Marquis Dubai** hotel, formerly the world's tallest hotel (355m/1165ft) until the nearby *Rose Rayhaan by Rotana* on Sheikh nabbed its record in 2018. The hotel occupies one of a soaring pair of identical blue-glass-clad towers whose strangely contoured outlines appear to be modelled on the trunk of a palm tree, each topped with a spiky little crown.

Opposite the *Marriott*, you can't fail to notice the **Iris Bay** building, an extraordinary crescent-shaped structure (like an eye turned sideways – hence the name), while back down the road, next to the intersection opposite the metro, stands the **Omniyat** tower, like an enormous popcorn carton made out of shiny black glass, and, next door, the **Prism** building, looking exactly as its name suggests.

East of here, **The Opus** is another work by Zaha Hadid, a huge, sinuously sculpted mass of dark glass, while further south lies the funky O-14 tower, popularly known as the **Swiss Cheese Tower** thanks to the undulating layer of white cladding which envelops the entire structure, dotted with around 1300 circular holes. The design is said to have been inspired by traditional Arabian-style *mashrabiya* wood carving, but actually looks more like an enormous piece of postmodern Emmenthal cheese.

The decorative interior of the Jumeirah Grand Mosque dome

JUMEIRAH

HIGHLIGHTS

» Southern Jumeirah, see page 67

Running parallel to Sheikh Zayed Road, Dubai's beach-fringed coastline begins just west of the old city centre, running to the border at the port and free-trade zone at Jebel Ali, some 32km (20 miles) distant. At the northern end of the beach strip, the upmarket but low-key suburb of **Jumeirah** is the closest coastal suburb to the old city centre, popular both with local Emiratis and wealthy expat workers.

The major tourist sight in Jumeirah is **Jumeirah Mosque ㉓**, at the northern end of Jumeirah Road. Built in the medieval Fatimid-style between 1975 and 1978, Jumeirah Mosque is one of the few in the city that non-Muslims are permitted to enter. Tours (www.jumeirahmosque.ae/mosque-visit-public; daily except Friday at 10am and 2pm) begin with entertaining and informative talks by a local Emirati guide on traditional religious practices, after which the floor is thrown open to questions, offering visitors a chance to quiz the guide on any aspect of local life. There's no need to book, but make sure you're at the mosque fifteen minutes before the tour starts and buy your ticket outside.

Just under 1km north of here at the top of Jumeirah Road, the striking **Etihad Museum ㉔** (Etihad being the Arabic word for "union") commemorates the foundation of the modern UAE, whose creation was ratified here back in 1971, ending over one hundred and fifty years of British stewardship. Designed to resemble a piece of folded paper, the striking modernist museum evokes the manuscript on which the agreement was signed, supported by seven columns symbolizing the pens used by the various emirates' seven rulers. Exhibits cover the modern history of the nation, focusing particularly on the period just before and after independence, with films, photos and artefacts commemorating the country's founders and the early years of its existence.

Standing in the museum grounds, **Union House** is where the agreement was actually signed – a quaint little circular structure now meticulously restored to its original condition after very nearly being knocked down in the 1990s.

Just south of Jumeriah Mosque, the stylish **La Mer** beachside development formerly offered a one-stop day-by-the-waves destination, with a fine swathe of sand equipped with changing huts and showers and a big selection of places to eat and drink, plus the obligatory slew of shops. The whole complex was being redeveloped as the **J1 Beach** complex at the time of writing, but may have opened by the time you read this.

SOUTHERN JUMEIRAH

Continuing down Jumeirah Road for another 2.5km, the fun, Italian-inspired **Mercato Mall** ㉕ (www.mercatoshoppingmall.com) looks like a kind of miniature medieval Italian city rebuilt by the Disney Corporation, with a series of brightly coloured quasi-Venetian-cum-Tuscan palazzi arranged around a huge central atrium overlooked by panoramic balconies and topped by a big glass roof.

Another 2.5km down Jumeirah Road, the sleepy suburban backstreets of Jumeirah provide the unlikely location of one of the Arabian Gulf's most significant ancient monuments, the **Jumeirah Archaeological Site**, where the ruins of a port town dating back more than one thousand years have been uncovered by archeologists since 1969. The original settlement, strategically positioned on the ancient trade route between Mesopotamia and Oman, dates back to the pre-Islamic Sassanid era, which ended in the seventh century AD. The site was built upon and expanded by the Abbasids in the first two

The Etihad Museum

A colourful sky over Kite Beach

or three centuries of the Islamic era and is today one of the largest and most important early Islamic sites in the Gulf. Excavated ruins include the foundations of several houses, including the Sassanid-era governor's palace, market buildings, a large caravanserai in which travellers would meet and do business, and a small mosque, although unfortunately they are all extremely fragmentary, and unlikely to mean much unless you are a trained archeologist. The site isn't currently open to the public, although you can get a decent view of the remains from the streets outside.

From here, it's around a further 1km south to Jumeirah's other sight of (albeit much more modern) historic interest, the time-warped **Majlis Ghorfat Umm al Sheif** ㉖. Built in 1955, when this part of the coast was far removed from the city on the creek, this modest two-storey coral-stone and gypsum building was used by

Sheikh Rashid as a meeting house before becoming a police station for a time in the 1960s. The house has now been turned into a small museum, while the grounds boast an example of the traditional *falaj* irrigation system and a *barasti* (palm frond) structure with a working wind-tower. It's located on Street 17, off Jumeirah Road – look for the brown heritage-site signs.

DUBAI WATER CANAL

HIGHLIGHTS

» The Jumeirah Corniche and beaches, see page 70
» Burj Al Arab and around, see page 71
» Mall of the Emirates, see page 75

Opened in 2017, the **Dubai Water Canal** heads inland from the southern end of Jumeirah (between the Jumeirah Archeological Site and Majlis al Ghorfat), running past Safa Park and then snaking between the skyscrapers of Business Bay (see page 64) before reaching Ras al Khor (see page 84), where it connects with the southern end of the Creek, forming an unbroken waterway encircling a significant portion of the central city. Starting in Jumeirah, a 6.4km walkway and cycle path runs along both sides of the canal, offering an enjoyably traffic-free place to stretch your legs or spin your wheels, with impressive skyscraper views en route plus a sequence of striking pedestrianized bridges including the ingenious Twisted Bridge and the graceful Bridge of Tolerance. Bike Shop Dubai (www.bikeshopdubai.com) in Business Bay is conveniently located for bike rentals, while **abra cruises** along the canal are available from Sheikh Zayed Road Marine Transport Station (45min–1hr; a minimum of eight passengers needed).

Tucked away by the canal a couple of blocks inland from the coast, **Safa Park** offers a refreshing expanse of grassy parkland, impressively backdropped by the skyscrapers of Sheikh Zayed Road. The park is well supplied with children's attractions, including numerous play areas, a boating lake and a miniature fairground area, although some attractions only operate in the evenings, if at all.

THE JUMEIRAH CORNICHE AND BEACHES

Dubai's coastline has been massively transformed over the past five years or so, with the creation of a long string of **public beaches** (all free; open 24hr) which now fringe most of the Jumeirah waterfront and then continue south almost all the way to the *Burj Al Arab* in the neighbouring suburb of Umm Suqeim. The entire waterfront is sometimes collectively referred to as the **Jumeirah Corniche**, although individual bits of beach go by an incomprehensible variety of interchangeable names. As well as huge expanses of sand, the Corniche also boasts excellent running and cycling tracks, lots of watersports and great views inland to Downtown Dubai and south to the *Burj Al Arab*.

The Corniche begins south of the Jumeirah Mosque, with a long strip of almost continuous sand – known variably as **Jumeirah Beach**, Jumeirah Public Beach or Jumeirah Open Beach – stretching down to the Dubai Water Canal. This stretch of coast is generally pretty quiet, and the sands usually fairly empty, particularly on weekdays, and with few facilities (unless you fancy diving into one of the Michelin-starred restaurants at the uber-luxurious *Bulgari* and *Four Seasons* hotels, which frame the southern end of the beach).

Things are generally a lot livelier south of the canal, starting with a pair of small semicircular beaches known as Nessnass Beach and Sunset Beach (after the nearby Sunset Mall). Slightly further south, **Kite Beach** 27 is where most of the action is, running from just past the Dubai Sailing Club all the way to the new *Marsa Al Arab* hotel. As the name suggests the area is particularly popular with kitesurfers, while wakeboarding and stand-up paddleboarding are also becoming popular and you can also surf – Surf House Dubai (www.surfingdubai.com) and Kitesurf School Dubai (www.kitesurf.

ae) can arrange all sorts of watersports and lessons to suit. It's also one of the few places you can go swimming after dark (there's a dedicated area towards the southern end of the beach just north of MGM Resort Island), with floodlit waters and evening lifeguards. There are also great views down the coast to the *Burj Al Arab* and other waterfront landmarks, although the classic view of the *Burj* itself from the southern end of the beach has now sadly been blocked off by the construction of the new *Marsa Al Arab* hotel.

BURJ AL ARAB AND AROUND

Towering above the coast at the southern end of Kite Beach, the **Burj Al Arab** ㉘ ("Tower of the Arabs") hotel has become the de facto symbol of the city since opening in 1999, its distinctive sail-shaped outline now almost as iconic as those of Big Ben or the Eiffel Tower. The 321m- (1,053ft-) high structure, shaped like a sail to complement the "wave" design of the nearby *Jumeirah Beach Hotel*, dominates the surrounding city and can be seen from virtually any point on the southern Dubai coast. Often described as the world's first "seven-star" hotel (although not, it must be said, by the hotel itself), the *Burj* is built on its own man-made island and covered in a distinctive Teflon-coated glass-fibre facade – white by day and beautifully illuminated in

The unmistakable Burj Al Arab

VISITING THE BURJ AL ARAB

Non-guests are only allowed into the *Burj* with a prior reservation on one of the hotel's various packages. The cheapest option is to sign up for a **guided tour** (www.insideburjalarab.com). Alternatively, make a reservation (tel: 800 32 32 32, email: restaurants@jumeirah.com) at one of the hotel's bars or restaurants. Big spenders might enjoy the hotel's two fine-dining restaurants: the *Ristorante L'Olivo at Al Mahara*, in a spectacular subterranean aquarium, or *Al Muntaha*, at the very top of the building, while there are several other slightly less wallet-draining dining options available – or have a drink or a sumptuous afternoon tea at either the *Sahn Eddar* lobby lounge or the *Skyview Bar*, perched next to *Al Muntaha* at the summit of the hotel. Other options include a visit to the gorgeous Talise spa or spending a day on the private beach terrace.

changing colours after dark. The distinctive helicopter pad jutting out from the top floor has the look of a mini *Starship Enterprise* and was famously used as a practice driving range by Tiger Woods and as a tennis court by Roger Federer and Andre Agassi.

On the beach right next to the *Burj* sits the second of the area's landmark buildings, the huge **Jumeirah Beach Hotel** ㉙ (or "JBH"). Designed to resemble an enormous breaking wave (although it looks more like an enormous roller coaster), and rising to a height of over 100m, the hotel was considered the most spectacular and luxurious in the city when it opened in 1997, although it has since been overtaken on both counts. It remains a fine sight, however, especially when seen from a distance in combination with the *Burj al Arab*, against whose slender sail it appears (with a little imagination) to be about to crash. Right next to the *JBH*, **Wild Wadi Water Park** has thirty rides and attractions, including the Jumeirah Sceirah, the tallest free-fall slide outside North America, and the Wipeout Flow Rider surf pool, where budding surfers can ride a continuously breaking 3m- (10ft-) high wave.

Immediately north of the *JBH* and opposite the *Burj Al Arab*, the **Jumeirah Marsa Al Arab** hotel is the newest of the area's landmark developments, completing the so-called "oceanic trilogy" of supersized luxury hotels inspired by the city's nautical past. The huge, superyacht-inspired outline echoes that of the *JBH*, complete with attached "pier" complex offering stunning views across the city's most spectacular architectural ensemble.

A stone's throw south along the coast lies the sprawling **Madinat Jumeirah** ㉚, a self-contained miniature "Arabian" city comprising a vast sprawl of sand-coloured buildings topped by an extraordinary quantity of wind towers (best viewed from the entrance to the *Al Qasr* hotel), the whole thing arranged around a sequence of meandering waterways along which visitors are chauffeured in replica abras.

Madinat Jumeirah resort: twenty-first-century luxury in traditional style

The vision, according to the developers, was "to recreate life as it used to be for residents along Dubai Creek, complete with waterways, abras, wind towers and a bustling souk", although in truth Madinat Jumeirah bears about as much relation to old Dubai as Big Ben does to your average grandfather clock. Even so, the sheer scale of the place, with its picturesque array of wind towers and palm-fringed waterways, is strangely compelling, and a perfect example of the kind of thing – mixing unbridled extravagance with a significant dose of sugar-coated kitsch – which Dubai seems to do so well. The Madinat also offers some of the most eye-boggling views in Dubai, with the futuristic outlines of the *Burj Al Arab* surreally framed between medieval-looking wind towers and Moorish arcading. The fact that the fake old-world city is actually newer

Hookahs at the Souk Madinat Jumeirah

than the ultramodern *Burj* is, by Dubai's standards, exactly what one would expect.

Much of the complex is taken up by pair of ultra-luxurious, Arabian themed five-star hotels (*Al Qasr* and *Mina A'Salam*), plus the very exclusive *Dar al Masyaf* resort and the idyllic Talise spa – while the newer *Jumeirah Al Naseem* hotel on the edge of the complex adds further five-star Arabian-themed lodgings with a more contemporary vibe. For casual visitors, however, the main attraction is the ridiculously pretty **Souk Madinat Jumeirah**, a gorgeous little labyrinth of wooden-roofed alleyways lined with upmarket souvenir shops and a good spread of places to eat and drink, particularly if you can bag a seat at one of the souk's waterfront establishments, offering beautiful views past the meandering canals and endless wind towers, with the vast outline of the *Burj Al Arab* rising surreally behind.

MALL OF THE EMIRATES

Around 2.5km inland from the *Burj Al Arab*, on Sheikh Zayed Road, the landmark **Mall of the Emirates** ㉛ (www.malloftheemirates.com) was formerly the largest in the city until being eclipsed by the Dubai Mall and is still one of the city's best places to shop – less exhaustingly huge than the Dubai Mall, but with almost five hundred shops covering pretty much every retail option.

Shopping aside, the Mall of the Emirates is best known as the home of **Ski Dubai** (www.skidxb.com; charge), the world's largest indoor snow park (and the only one in the Middle East), complete with regular falls of artificial snow and an alpine ski slope offering five runs of varying levels of difficulty – a truly surreal experience in the middle of the desert, and a great place to cool off when the mercury is touching 48°C (118°F) outside.

Around 1km north of the Mall of the Emirates, on the desert side of the highway near Interchange No. 4, the functional **Gold and Diamond Park** (www.goldanddiamondpark.com) lacks the atmosphere of the city's traditional souks but offers some of the cheapest gold and precious stones in the city – diamonds are a particularly good buy.

THE PALM JUMEIRAH AND DUBAI MARINA

HIGHLIGHTS

- Atlantis, see page 76
- The rest of the Palm, see page 79
- Dubai Marina, see page 80
- Ibn Battuta Mall, see page 82
- Expo City Dubai, see page 82

South of Madinat Jumeirah in the suburb of Al Sufouh, a multi-lane highway branches off the coastal highway to head out to sea and the remarkable **Palm Jumeirah,** one of the world's largest man-made islands, reclaimed between 2001 and 2006 and stretching 4km out into the waters of the Arabian Gulf.

As its name implies, the island is designed in the form of a palm tree, with the main road running down the central "trunk", a series of sixteen "fronds" spreading out to either side, covered in luxury villas, and an outer breakwater lined with upmarket hotels. Unfortunately, you can only really appreciate the unique layout of the island from the air; from the ground, the whole thing looks like suburban clutter, while the architecture along the main trunk road is decidedly humdrum, at least until you approach the far end of the island, and the grandiose *Atlantis* resort heaves into view ahead.

ATLANTIS

At the far end of the Palm, the vast **Atlantis resort** ㉜ rears into view above the seafront (www.atlantisthepalm.com). Looking like some enormous Disney palace, the resort is an almost identikit

Atlantis resort

copy of its sister establishment, the *Atlantis Paradise Island* resort in the Bahamas, with the addition of the few discrete Islamic touches. Inside, the hotel is as unabashedly over-the-top as one would expect. Entering the main foyer, you're confronted by Dale Chihuly's extraordinary installation: a towering glass sculpture looking like a huge waterfall of deep-frozen spaghetti. Corridors stretch away in either direction, lined with fat gold columns and vast chandeliers, and a floor-to-ceiling viewing panel offers spectacular glimpses into the vast aquarium of the hotel's Lost Chambers.

The kooky **Lost Chambers** purports to consist of the remains of the legendary city of *Atlantis*, featuring a sequence of underwater halls and tunnels, dotted with specially constructed "ruins". You may enjoy the sheer absurdity of the idea, and the 65,000-odd

THE WORLD

Lying around 5km off the coast, **The World** development comprises a fanciful archipelago of artificial islands constructed in the shape of an approximate map of the world (weirdly impressive when seen from the air). It was originally hoped that developers would buy up individual islands and create themed tourist developments, perhaps based on the "nationality" of the island they occupy. Physical reclamation of the islands was completed in around 2006, but it's only in the last few years that any significant development has occurred, centred on The Heart of Europe (www.thoe.com), spread across six islands in the "Europe" section of the archipelago and featuring a cluster of funky hotels, wacky floating villas and "the world's first temperature-controlled street". There's also the very upmarket Anantara World Islands Resort (at the southern tip of "South America"), plus a low-key beach club on Lebanon Island (www.theisland.ae). Whether these new developments will finally kickstart the project into life remains to be seen, however, and for the time being the remainder of the archipelago's islands remain uninhabited – and apparently unloved – dots of sand in the ocean.

resident fish, both large and small, swimming around the submerged faux-classical remains.

In the grounds outside you'll find the resort's spectacular **Aquaventure Waterpark**, home to a pulse-quickening selection of water-coasters, speed slides and power-jets, plus the dramatic Ziggurat "Leap of Faith" waterslide, which drops those brave enough to tackle it, at a stomach-churning speed, down a plastic tunnel into the middle of a lagoon full of sharks. There are also various gentler activities for kids (including a children's play area), while visitors can also use the fine stretch of private beach next door. The adjacent **Dolphin Bay** offers the chance to swim with the hotel's troupe of resident bottlenose dolphins, although as with similar projects across the Gulf (and indeed worldwide) the attraction has raised serious ethical concerns.

THE REST OF THE PALM

Despite its grandiose design, much of the Palm is rather humdrum at ground level. Most interesting is the outer **Crescent**, lined with a sequence of overblown mega-hotels. Many of these are still under construction, and most of those which have got finished are pretty darn ugly, although brief visual relief is provided by the cod-Moorish *Jumeirah Zabeel Saray*, the quirky *Wyndham Residencies* (modelled after the mudbrick "skyscrapers" of the Yemeni capital Sanaa) and, especially, the uber-luxurious new **Atlantis, The Royal** resort (next door to the original *Atlantis* resort), looking like a vast heap of post-modern Jenga bricks piled high into the sky. Running alongside the road around the entire Crescent, the **Palm Jumeirah Boardwalk** is popular with walkers and joggers towards dusk, although rather hot during the day, given the complete lack of shade.

Dubai Marina

NOTES

The best way to see the Palm is from the **Palm Monorail**, whose driverless trains shuttle along an elevated track between *Atlantis* and Gateway station on the mainland, taking around ten minutes to complete the trip – a fine ride offering sweeping views over the Palm and beyond. The monorail connects to Palm Jumeirah station on the Dubai Tram network (it's a five-minute walk between the monorail and tram stations, clearly signed through a multistorey car park). Intermediate stations serve Nakheel Mall and Al Ittihad Park (for Palm West Beach).

Elsewhere, specific attractions are fairly thin on the ground. Most visitors head to the 1.6km-long **Palm West Beach** (a two-minute walk from Al Ittihad Park monorail station), offering an expansive swathe of free sand, great views of the marina and assorted places to eat. Nearby, the shiny new **Nakheel Mall** is the Palm's main retail hub, while perched atop the attached Palm Tower, **The View at the Palm** observation deck (www.theviewpalm.ae; charge) offers superb views of the Palm itself and the southern city beyond.

DUBAI MARINA

Past the turn-off to the Palm rise the massed buildings of the vast Dubai Marina development. This entire district is effectively a brand new city-within-the-city: a swathe of densely packed skyscrapers which mushroomed out of the desert with magical rapidity over little more than five years during the late noughties. Even by Dubai standards, the speed and scale of the development here takes your breath away, especially for those who remember this part of Dubai in its pre-2005 days, when the entire area was little more than untouched desert, bar a modest line of hotels fringing the coast.

These upmarket beachside hotels remain the Marina's principal tourist draw, lining the long expanse of fine white-sand beach on the western side of the area. The hotel strip begins at its eastern end with the Arabian-themed **One&Only Royal Mirage** ❸❸, one of the city's loveliest hotels, followed in rapid succession by the *Meridien Mina Seyahi* and *Westin* hotels.

Past here the main road drops over the sea inlet leading into Dubai Marina itself to reach **The Walk** ❸❹, an attractive pedestrianized promenade running along the back of the beach, dotted with dozens of cafés and restaurants. Bounding the ocean-side of The Walk, **The Beach at JBR** leisure complex (www.thebeach.ae) comprises an attractive cluster of low-rise buildings with crisp, quasi-Bauhaus lines arranged around a quartet of pretty piazzas – one of Dubai's more modest but most successful retail and leisure developments.

Facing the Marina on Bluewaters Island is **Ain Dubai** ("Dubai Eye"), one of the southern city's most visible landmarks. Almost a carbon-copy of the older London Eye, albeit almost twice as tall (250m), this is – or at least was – the world's tallest Ferris wheel, although it was "temporarily" closed in March 2022 and had yet to reopen as of 2024, with rumours suggesting that the wheel's main axle had broken, or that the foundations themselves were subsiding.

A short walk inland from here, the **Marina** itself is a man-made sea inlet, around

A monumental water feature at Expo 2020

1.5km (1 mile) long, dotted with luxury yachts and fancy speedboats, with the waters hemmed in by a forest of skyscrapers. It's an impressive sight, although the haphazard layout of the entire area, with random high-rises crammed pell-mell into every available space, is a reminder of the mad rush with which the entire area was created.

IBN BATTUTA MALL

Some 4km (2.5 miles) south of the Marina lies the quirky **Ibn Battuta Mall** ㉟ (www.ibnbattutamall.com), situated in something of a no-man's land at the far southern end of the city, close to the sprawling industrial works and container docks of the Jebel Ali Free Trade Zone. The mall is one of the city's most outlandish but engaging attractions, inspired by the travels of the famous Moroccan wanderer Ibn Battuta, with different sections themed after six of the many countries and regions he visited – Morocco, Andalusia, Tunisia, Persia, India and China – all designed with Dubai's characteristic mix of whimsy, extravagance and high kitsch.

EXPO CITY DUBAI

The ground-breaking **Dubai Expo 2020** (although it was actually held in 2021–22 due to Covid) was one of most spectacular in the history of the global exhibition series and the first ever held in the Middle East, transforming over four square kilometres of former desert at the southern edge of Dubai into a futuristic hub at a cost of around US$8 billion. Several of the Expo's largest structures have been left in place and are now being repurposed as **Expo City Dubai** (www.expocitydubai.com), a major new commercial, conference and tourist hub – although the entire area is still currently very much a work in progress.

Centrepiece of the development is the flagship **Al Wasl Plaza**, enclosed in a cavernous metallic dome. Serenely silver by the day, the dome transforms after dark into an incredible 360-degree screen, with pictures projected by over two hundred and fifty lasers conjuring up a dazzling, ever-changing array of kaleidoscopic images – anything from traditional Islamic architectural interiors to shoals of tropical fish. Other highlights include the dramatic **Alif Mobility Pavilion** by Foster + Partners, and the flying-saucer-shaped **Terra** "sustainability pavilion", designed to be entirely energy self-sufficient even in Dubai's challenging climate. The building's huge canopy harvests sunlight, rainwater and dew, while further solar power is generated by the surrounding cluster of "energy trees", which track the sun daily for optimum effect. Look out too for the aptly named *Surreal* (a kind of fountain which flows upwards), and the Garden in the Sky observation tower, aka "The Flying Park".

The Ain Dubai ("Dubai Eye") on Bluewaters Island

AWAY FROM THE COAST

HIGHLIGHTS

- Ras al Khor Wildlife Sanctuary, see page 84
- Dubai Safari Park, see page 84
- Dubailand, see page 85
- Dubai Park and Resort, see page 86

RAS AL KHOR WILDLIFE SANCTUARY

Close to Nad Al Sheba, the tidal lagoon at the top of Dubai Creek is home to the UAE's largest bird sanctuary, **Ras al Khor Wildlife Sanctuary** ㊱, which can host up to fifteen thousand birds on a single winter's day, including between 1000 and 1500 migrant greater flamingos, a protected species here since 1985. Other species that can be seen from the purpose-built viewing hides on Route 66 and Ras al Khor Road (Route 44) include Socotra cormorants, cream-coloured coursers and crab plovers.

DUBAI SAFARI PARK

Opened in 2017, the **Dubai Safari Park** (www.dubaisafari.ae) provides a new home for the thousand-odd animals formerly incarcerated in the horribly cramped old Dubai Zoo in Jumeirah, who now rub shoulders with around two thousand more recent arrivals in this state-of-the-art complex. The park's three main areas are devoted to the wildlife of Africa, Asia and Arabia respectively, arranged around the artificial Al Wadi mini-river and featuring a mix of traditional walk-through zoo enclosures and tanks alongside open drive-through sections for big cats and other larger species. Visits to the drive-through

RELIGIOUS TOLERANCE

According to the Sheikh Mohammed Centre for Cultural Understanding (see page), "cultural and religious diversity has made the Emirates probably the most open and tolerant country within the region. Dubai and the UAE in general are liberal in allowing foreigners to maintain their own religious practices and lifestyles".

Although Emiratis are Muslims and the legal system that applies to locals and foreigners alike is based on Islamic Sharia Law, the Dubai government allows people of other faiths to gather for worship, as long as they don't proselytize Muslims, and a number of Christian churches have been established on land provided by the rulers on the Bur Dubai side of the Creek.

sections are on the park's large-ish buses, so it's not exactly your classic African jeep safari, but still reasonable fun, especially if you've got kids in tow.

Racing at the Autodrome

DUBAILAND

Occupying a huge swathe of land some 10km inland from the marina, the vast **Dubailand** development was the defining symbol of the spectacular hubris which engulfed the entire city for much of the noughties. Launched in 2003, Dubailand was originally slated to become the planet's largest and most spectacular tourist development, costing an estimated US$65 billion and boasting an extraordinary mix of theme parks and sporting and leisure facilities covering a staggering 280 square kilometres – twice the size of Walt Disney World in Florida.

In the event, Dubailand struggled from day one, while many of the proposed elements of the original plan were finished off completely by the financial crisis of 2008 (along with most of the emirate's other loopier mega-projects – underwater hotel, anyone?). Parts of the original masterplan did actually manage to get built, however, with a smattering of attractions dotted across the desert amidst swathes of new housing developments. These include the **Dubai Outlet Mall, Global Village** (see page 105), the **Dubai Autodrome** (www.dubaiautodrome.com), a 5.39km Formula One-standard motor-racing circuit which hosts rounds of the FIA GT Championship, **Dubai**

Sports City ㊲ (www.dsc.ae), complete with international cricket stadium, plus a quartet of **golf courses** (the Els, the Arabian Ranches, and the "Earth" and "Fire" courses at Jumeirah Golf Estates), while other attractions have since emerged to fill at least some of the gaps.

One of the few original Dubailand novelty attractions which actually got finished, the **Dubai Miracle Garden** (www.dubaimiracle garden.com) is claimed to be the world's largest flower garden (complete with an alleged 45 million plants), although the place is notable not so much for its record-breaking botanical contents as for the sheer zaniness of the overall design – a surreal horticultural head trip complete with striped flower beds, wacky topiary and myriad outlandish designs (changed annually) which have previously included floral pyramids, flower-encrusted buildings and cars, an 18m-high floral replica of the Burj Khalifa, and an Emirates Airbus A380 plane. The attached **Butterfly Garden** (www.dubaibutterflygarden.com) seems rather tame in comparison, with fifteen thousand of the winged creatures flitting around nine climate-controlled domes.

DUBAI PARK AND RESORT

In the far south of the city, **Dubai Parks and Resorts** offers a fun day out – in fact several fun days out – for all the family. Situated around 20km south of Dubai Marina, about halfway to Abu Dhabi, the development comprises a trio of theme parks plus the **Riverland Dubai** dining and retail development (www.riverlanddubai.com), complete with faux-French "medieval" village, the ersatz-Mughal India Gate and the retro 1950s-style Americana-themed Boardwalk complex.

Star of the show is the spectacular **Motiongate Dubai** (www.motiongatedubai.com/en), a kind of Universal Studios/Disneyland-style theme park featuring rides and attractions based on films and characters by DreamWorks Animation, Columbia Pictures and Lionsgate. **Bollywood Parks Dubai** (www.visitbollywoodpark.com) follows a similar theme, aimed firmly at the region's subcontinental residents and visitors, while the adjacent **Legoland** and

Legoland Water Park (www.legoland.com/dubai) serve up the usual blocktastic rides and entertainments found at the company's other theme parks worldwide.

DAY TRIPS

HIGHLIGHTS

- The desert, see page 88
- Hatta, see page 88
- Sharjah, see page 89
- Al Ain, see page 90
- The east coast, see page 90
- Abu Dhabi, see page 91

Hatta Heritage Village, built around an ancient settlement

THE DESERT

The dunes that begin on the outskirts of the city continue into Abu Dhabi Emirate and eventually merge with the fabled Rub Al Khali, or Empty Quarter, the largest sand desert in the world, with some sand dunes reaching 300m (985ft). Encroaching development means, admittedly, that the sands surrounding Dubai are far from pristine, although half-day "sunset safaris" (run by pretty much every tour agent in the city: see page 98) offer a fun, if slightly cheesy, chance to at least sample something of this austerely beautiful environment.

Several companies also offer longer and more interesting desert excursions. Easily the most rewarding destination is the **Dubai Desert Conservation Reserve** (www.ddcr.org), a picture-perfect area of desert protecting 250 square kilometres of shifting dunes, dotted with stunted acacia, firebush and indigenous *ghaf* trees which is home to rare and endangered creatures including oryx, Arabian mountain gazelle, sand gazelle, Arabian red fox and sand fox.

HATTA

The Dubai enclave of **Hatta** ㊳, on the highway 115km (71 miles) from the city, can be reached by car in slightly over an hour. Hatta's appeal lies in the contrast of its oasis greenery and rugged mountain backdrop, but its main visitor attraction is undoubtedly **Hatta Heritage Village**, which traces the history of the settlement from its formation some three thousand years ago to the nineteenth century and has examples of thirty traditional structures, from a fortress built by Sheikh Maktoum Bin Hasher Al Maktoum in 1896 to small mountain dwellings that wouldn't look out of place on the islands off the Scottish coast. The two round defensive watchtowers on either side of the heritage village, also built in the 1880s, offer some spectacular views of the museum and the modern town.

Sheikh Zayed Grand Mosque in Abu Dhabi

SHARJAH

On the coast north of Dubai lies **Sharjah** ㊴, once the most important town on the Trucial Coast, but now overshadowed by its more glamorous neighbour. Nevertheless, Sharjah has a number of attractions to justify the trip out from Dubai. In the centre of town, the Creekside **heritage area** is home to several small museums and the pretty little Al Arsa Souk, while just down the road lie the old city **fort**, the **Sharjah Art Gallery** and the outstanding **Sharjah Museum of Islamic Civilization** (www.sharjahmuseums.ae). Slightly out from the centre, the landmark **Blue Souk** is home to a good selection of carpet and handicrafts shops, while the nearby aviation-themed **Al Mahatta Museum** (www.sharjahmuseums.ae) occupies the site of the former airport, established in 1932 to serve the pioneering Imperial Airways route between Croydon, England and Australia.

AL AIN

The attractive city of Al Ain – the UAE's largest inland settlement – offers a rewarding day trip from Dubai, an easy 90-minute journey along the swift E66 highway. The greenest city in the UAE, Al Ain grew up around the string of seven oases that survive to this day; the largest, right in the heart of the city, makes for a beautifully peaceful and shaded walk along narrow lanes threading their way between endless lines of date palms. The city is also famous for its fine collection of traditional mudbrick forts, including the striking **Al Jahili Fort** (http://bit.ly/JahiliFort) and the rustic little Sultan Zayed Fort, which stands next to the Al Ain National Museum (currently closed for renovations). The lively **Camel Souk** (http://bit.ly/CamelSouk) on the edge of town is also worth a visit, as is the breezy summit of the craggy Jebel Hafeet mountain, rising to the south of the city.

Beach resort in Fujairah

THE EAST COAST

On the east coast of the UAE, around two-hours' drive from Dubai, the highway from Masafi to Fujairah passes **Bithnah Fort**, which in its mountain oasis setting is reminiscent of the great forts of northern Oman. **Fujairah** also has an imposing fortress with a mountain backdrop. The fort, attacked by British forces in colonial times, is believed to be the oldest in the UAE, dating back five hundred years.

The UAE's oldest mosque, built around 1446, is on the coast 38km (24 miles) north of Fujairah at **Badiyah** (non-Muslims are usually allowed in outside prayer times). A short drive further north is the gorgeous **Al Aqah Beach** ⓸⓪, a popular weekend retreat for Dubai residents, with a trio of upmarket hotels, including the landmark **Le Meridien al Aqah Beach Resort**. The clear, warm waters around nearby **Snoopy Island** are particularly popular with scuba divers and snorkellers.

ABU DHABI

A quick two-hour drive down the coast, the wealthy capital of the UAE, **Abu Dhabi** ⓸⓵ is considerably more staid than its upstart neighbour Dubai but still offers a good selection of attractive beaches, swanky hotels and a growing number of landmark attractions. The major sight here is the vast **Sheikh Zayed Mosque** (www.szgmc.gov.ae), completed in 2007 and one of the largest and most lavishly decorated places of worship anywhere in the world.

The city's other major landmark development is currently **Saadiyat Island** (www.saadiyat.ae), home to the stunning **Louvre Abu Dhabi** (www.louvreabudhabi.ae; charge) designed by French architect Jean Nouvel, opened in 2017 and showcasing a fine collection of both Eastern and Western art. Two further mega-museums – Norman Foster's **Sheikh Zayed National Museum** and Frank Gehry's **Guggenheim Abu Dhabi** – are also currently under construction and due to open in 2025, but don't hold your breath.

In the centre of town, the sprawling old **Qasr al Hosn** fort, the oldest building in Abu Dhabi (www.qasralhosn.ae; charge), hosts interesting displays on the history of the city, while it's also worth a look at the nearby **World Trade Centre** (www.wtcad.ae): a stunning, postmodern souk designed by Norman Foster. Finally, on the western side of town rises the vast, palatial **Emirates Palace** hotel (www.mandarinoriental.com) and, sitting alongside, the similarly opulent **Qasr al Watan** presidential palace (www.qasralwatan.ae; charge).

On a desert safari

Things to do

There's a huge array of things to do in Dubai. Outdoor activities range from classic desert safaris through to watersports, cycling and golf, and there's also a good selection of premier sporting events to enjoy, along with loads of other annual festivals focusing on anything from film and jazz to traditional Emirati culture. Dubai's vibrant clubbing scene is another draw, as are the city's myriad shopping opportunities, from atmospheric souks to swanky malls – or you could just chill in one of the city's idyllic spas. Cultural attractions are, admittedly, rather thin on the ground, although a couple of large-scale venues host regular international acts and city's thriving visual arts scene is amongst the best in the region.

CULTURE

Dubai is widely derided as a city that culture forgot, and in truth there's a dearth of decent theatres, performing venues or independent cinemas, while even now the city's musical life is largely limited to the occasional big-name visiting acts – although things do look up briefly during the excellent Dubai jazz and film festivals.

With a capacity of fifteen thousand, the outdoor Dubai Media City Amphitheatre (check www.timeoutdubai.com for details of forthcoming events) is the city's main venue for big shows by visiting international **music** acts (and also hosts the annual Dubai International Jazz Festival), while global stars also perform regularly at the funky new Coca-Cola Arena (www.coca-cola-arena.com). The landmark new Dubai Opera (www.dubaiopera.com) looks fabulous, although sadly there's very little actual opera on offer, with most performances featuring pitiful servings of cliched film music, plus assorted jazz and comedy acts.

For **cinema**, Dubai is well equipped with a string of modern multiplexes serving up all the latest Hollywood blockbusters, plus a few Bollywood flicks and the occasional Arabic film – although screenings

Al Mahara restaurant in the Burj Al Arab

of alternative and arthouse cinema are rare outside the excellent Dubai International Film Festival. Vox is the city's largest and most modern chain, with cinemas citywide including the flagship Mall of the Emirates branch boasting IMAX and 4DX screens. Dedicated cineastes will want to head to Cinema Akil in Al Quoz (www.cinemaakil.com), the city's only proper arthouse cinema, screening a constantly changing selection of off-beat films from across the globe.

Where Dubai has scored a major success is in establishing itself as the Gulf's **visual arts** capital, boasting a remarkable number of independent galleries, many set up by expats from around the Arab world and showcasing a healthy spread of cutting-edge work by a range of international artists. The city also hosts two big annual arts festivals in mid-March, when Art Dubai and the SIKKA Art Festival hit town.

The unlikely hub of the city's arts scene is the run-down industrial area of **Al Quoz**, off Sheikh Zayed Road in the southern city, whose low rents have attracted a string of gallery owners from across the Arab world. Many are located in the impressive Alserkal Avenue (www.alserkal.online), a dedicated arts complex housed in a converted warehouse. Leading, venues include the Beirut-based Ayyam gallery (www.ayyamgallery.com) and the venerable Green Art Gallery (www.gagallery.com), one of the oldest in the city, while the more cutting-edge and experimental Gallery Isabelle van den Eynde (www.ivde.net) and The Third Line (www.thethirdline.com) are also well worth a look.

There's a further cluster of more upmarket galleries in the **Gate Village** at the DIFC, most notably Artsawa (www.artsawa.com) and Tabari Artspace (www.tabariartspace.com), while back in the **old city**, Bur Dubai is home to the Majlis Gallery (www.themajlisgallery.com) and the XVA Gallery (www.xvagallery.com), both located in traditional buildings in Al Fahidi and amongst the city's oldest and most beautiful exhibition spaces.

NIGHTLIFE

Like pretty much everywhere else in the Gulf, Dubai only really gets going in the cooler evening and night-time hours. The city's vibrant nightlife takes many forms. Western expats and tourists tend to make for the city's restaurants, bars and clubs (for more on drinking, see page 116), while locals and expat Arabs can be found relaxing in the city's myriad

NOTES

During the holy month of Ramadan, eating and drinking in public (which includes smoking and chewing gum) are forbidden during daylight hours, and although hotels serve guests food and drink in curtained-off areas, no alcohol is served anywhere until after dark. The city's nightlife also grinds to a halt: live music is banned and clubs close for the duration.

Rooftop bar and wind-tower

shisha cafés. Souks and shopping malls across the city fill up with crowds of consumers from all walks of Dubai society – most remain remarkably busy right up to when they close around midnight, while clubs and some bars kick on until deep into the small hours.

Dubai has a huge **clubbing** scene, driven by a mix of western expats and tourists along with the city's large expat Arab (particularly Lebanese) community. Music tends to be a fairly mainstream selection of house, hip-hop and r'n'b (perhaps with a splash of Arabic pop), with a healthy number of visiting international DJs. The emphasis at more upmarket places still tends to be on posing and pouting – expect to see lots of beautiful young things from Beirut or Bombay quaffing champagne – although there's more fashion-free and egalitarian clubbing to be had at the city's big superclubs.

Venues come and go regularly, so it's worth checking the latest **listings** in *Time Out Dubai* (www.timeoutdubai.com) or visiting www.platinumlist.net to find out what's new and happening. Entrance **charges** generally vary depending on who's playing; entrance is sometimes free (if only for women); men can expect to pay 50–100dh. Most places also have a **couples-only policy** (which may or may not be enforced depending on how busy they are) – in general it's also worth dressing to impress, or prepare to be turned away. Quite a few **bars** also have regular live DJs and a club-like ambience later at night, particularly if there's a special event on.

Leading venues include *Sky2.0* in Dubai Design District (www.skydubai.com), a huge open-air superclub and one of the city's most spectacular outdoor spaces, and *WHITE* at Dubai Harbour (www.instagram.com/whitedubai), the city's other headline superclub, attracting leading international DJs and one of the city's most eclectic crowds. Smaller venues to look out for include *BO18* in Dubai Media City (www.b018dxb.com), an offshoot of the famous Lebanese venue and Winner of Time Out Dubai's Best Club in Dubai award in 2022, and the posy *ICY* on Sheikh Zayed Road (www.icydubai.com), allegedly "the most technologically advanced nightclub in Dubai".

For an authentic Arabian alternative to the pub, club or bar, nothing beats a visit to one of Dubai's **shisha cafés**, with local Emiratis and expat Arabs lounging around over endless cups of coffee while puffing away on a shisha (waterpipe). The best places

NOTES

Ladies Nights are a Dubai institution. These are usually held on Wednesday, Thursday or, most commonly, Tuesday nights in an attempt to drum up custom during the quieter midweek evenings, with lots of places around the city offering all sorts of deals for women, ranging from a couple of free cocktails up to complimentary champagne all night.

Dubai is home to the Middle East's only indoor ski slope

will have twenty or more varieties to choose from. Fancier shisha joints include the upmarket *Huqqa* in Dubai Mall (www.huqqa.com), with gorgeous views of the Dubai Fountains and Souk al Bahar, plus quality Turkish food, and the very chilled *Smoky Beach* at Dubai Marina (www.facebook.com/smokybeach), probably the only place in Dubai where you can smoke shisha on the beach at four in the morning. Or head to one of the two magical *The Courtyards* at the *One&Only Royal Mirage* hotel (www.royalmirage.oneandonlyresorts.com), occupying a pair of beautiful Moroccan-style courtyards complete with fairy-lit palms and *majlis*-style seating on big floor cushions.

OUTDOOR ACTIVITIES

One thing that virtually every visitor to Dubai does at some point is go on a **desert safari**. Most people opt for one of the ever-popular half-day safaris (also known as "sunset safaris"), although some operators offer overnight and full-day safaris if you want to get more of a feel for the desert. Tours are generally in large 4WDs holding around eight passengers. Sunset safaris begin around 3–4pm, starting with a 45min drive out into the desert. Here you'll be given a taste of the traditional Emirati pastime of dune-bashing, driving at high speed up and down increasingly precipitous dunes amid great sprays of sand while your vehicle slides, skids, bumps and occasionally takes off completely. You might also be given the chance to try your hand at a brief bit of **sand-skiing** or the chance to ride a quad bike (aka "dune buggy") across the dunes.

As dusk falls, you'll be taken to a so-called "**Bedouin camp**" in the desert, usually with various tents rigged up around a sandy enclosure and belly-dancing stage. Activities here include (very short) camel rides, henna painting, dressing up in Gulf national costume and having your photo taken with an Emirati falcon perched on your arm. A passable international buffet dinner is then served, after which a belly dancer usually performs for another half-hour or so. The whole thing winds up at around 9.30pm, then you'll be driven back to Dubai.

There's a growing selection of **watersports** available at many of the beachside hotels and through operators at the Marina beach including Sky & Sea (www.watersportsdubai.com) and Water Adventure Dubai (www.

NOTES

Dubai's ruling family has become synonymous with international horse racing, thanks mostly to the success of the Godolphin stable (www.godolphin.com), established by Sheikh Mohammed in 1994 – despite a massive doping scandal which rocked the stable's reputation back in 2013, when 22 horses at their Newmarket stables were found to have been dosed with anabolic steroids. Godolphin now have over one thousand five hundred horses in training across the globe and have won more than five thousand races in fourteen different countries, becoming one of the biggest buyers and breeders of racehorses on the planet, with a total investment in bloodstock, stud farms and various related properties now worth over US$2.5 billion.

wateradventure.ae). Typical offerings include sailing, windsurfing, kayaking, banana-boating, wakeboarding and deep-sea fishing. Kite Beach, as its name suggests, offers good kitesurfing, plus wakeboarding, stand-up paddleboarding and surfing. Operators include Kitesurf School Dubai (www.kitesurf.ae) and Surf House Dubai (www.surfingdubai.com).

Dubai itself has only limited **diving** opportunities but does lie within easy striking distance of outstanding dive sites off the UAE's east coast in Fujairah, and off the Musandam Peninsula in Oman. Leading operators include Al Boom Diving (www.alboomdiving.com) and the Bermuda Diving Centre (www.scubadiving.ae).

Golf is big business in Dubai, and the city has an outstanding selection of international-standard courses, generally at sky-high

The Dubai World Cup is horse racing's richest prize

prices – players on a budget should head to the (relatively) affordable nine-hole Jebel Ali Golf Resort (www.jaresortshotels.com). Leading venues include the long-running Dubai Creek Golf Club (www.dubaigolf.com) and the famous Emirates Golf Club (www.dubaigolf.com), home of the Dubai Desert Classic tournament. The beautiful Desert Course at Arabian Ranches (www.arabianranchesgolfclub.com) offers a more unusual alternative, with a grass links-style course set in the middle of natural desert.

Cycling has become increasingly popular in recent years, with the opening of an extensive network of high-quality cycle paths in various parts of the city. These include purpose-built cycle tracks along the Dubai Water Canal and Jumeirah Beach/Kite Beach, and various other city locations, while further afield there are also dedicated tracks out in the desert at Al Qudra and in the mountains at Hatta. For details of the various tracks see www.cyclingtracks.ae or www.dubairoadsters.com. Leading hire outlets

NOTES

Dubai has a vast collection of fabulous **spas** (most attached to hotels), offering just about every treatment you can imagine, and several you can't. Leading destinations include the gorgeous Arabian-themed Amara (www.dubaicreekresort.com/amara-spa) and The Palace (www.addresshotels.com) spas, while the gorgeous One&Only Spa (www.oneandonlyresorts.com) has one of the most picture-perfect hammams you'll ever see. Other sense-calming oases include the two vast Talise spas (www.jumeirah.com), at the *Jumeirah Zabeel Saray* hotel and in Madinat Jumeirah, and the unusual Tibetan-themed B/Attitude (www.battitudespa-dubai.com), with its seductive charm. Less pricey treatments can be found at the excellent Cleopatra's in the Wafi complex (www.cleopatrasspaandwellness.com).

include Wolfi's Bike Shop on Sheikh Zayed Road (www.wolfis.ae) and Bike Shop Dubai in Business Bay (www.bikeshopdubai.com). Note that cycling is illegal on "major" roads – defined as any road with a speed limit of over 60km/h.

Helicopter tours offer peerless (albeit pricey) views, with operators including Helicopter Tour Dubai (www.helicoptertourdubai.com) and Dubai Helicopter Tour (www.helicoptertour.ae). Alternatively, take to the air above southern Dubai and the Palm Jumeirah at **Skydive Dubai** (www.skydivedubai.ae), Dubai's ultimate adrenaline rush. More sedate **balloon** rides over the desert near Al Ain are run by Balloon Adventures Dubai (www.balloon-adventures.com).

Dubai and neighbouring Abu Dhabi also boast a surprisingly good selection of annual **sporting events**, attracting top names in a range of sports. Leading golfing events include the Dubai Desert (www.dubaidesertclassic.com; Jan), one of the most important dates in the PGA European Golf Tour, and the Dubai World Tour Championship (www.dpwtc.com; Nov), the showpiece finale of the European Tour's season-long "Race to Dubai". The world's tennis elite rocks up for the annual Dubai Duty Free Tennis Championships (www.dubaidutyfreetennischampionships.com; late Feb), while down in Abu Dhabi the Abu Dhabi Grand Prix (www.

The glittering Dubai Mall

yasmarinacircuit.com; Nov) is now an established fixture on the Formula 1 racing calendar.

Other events include the Dubai Marathon (www.dubaimarathon.org; Jan) and the UAE Tour (www.theuaetour.com; Feb), Dubai's answer to the Tour de France, while March sees the Dubai World Cup at the Meydan Racecourse (www.dubairacingclub.com), the world's richest horse race. There's also the much-loved Dubai Sevens (www.dubairugby7s.com; Nov/Dec), one of the highlights of the international rugby sevens calendar, while a programme of traditional dhow racing at the Dubai International Marine Club (www.dimc.ae; Feb) offers a rare opportunity to see the Gulf's traditional wooden dhows under sail. Or for a real taste of authentic Emirati culture, head to Al Marmoum Race Track, around 40km from Dubai off the Al Ain Rd (www.dcrc.ae, tel: 04 718 8888), one of the country's best places to see traditional camel racing, with races held from Oct to April from around 6–9am, although there's no fixed schedule. For details of forthcoming meets, call the racetrack on the number above. Entrance is free.

SHOPPING

Home to the world's largest mall and its oldest and biggest shopping festival, Dubai is a place which takes its retail therapy very seriously indeed. Dozens of spectacular modern malls dot the city, some of them virtual tourist attractions in their own right, while more traditional crafts can be found in the city's myriad souks.

WHERE TO BUY

The **souks** of the old city centre offer Dubai's most quintessential shopping, with goods piled high in tiny shops around twisting alleyways. The Gold Souk in Deira is the most famous, merging seamlessly into the adjacent Spice and Perfume souks. Across the Creek, Bur Dubai Souk is the place for textiles, while down-at-heel Karama Souk remains a great place to pick up designer fakes, cheap clothes and souvenirs. Most places open daily from 10am to 10pm, though some close in the afternoon and others don't open on Friday mornings. Bargaining is expected – ask for the "best price". For a modern remake of the traditional Arabian souk, head either to the lovely Souk Madinat Jumeirah or the opulent Khan Murjan Souk, both of which boast lavish decor and an Arabian Nights atmosphere – although prices are higher than in the old city centre souks.

Dubai's myriad **malls** (similarly, most open daily 10am–10pm) offer some of the most spectacular shopping on the planet. For pure retail excess, the supersized Dubai Mall (www.thedubaimall.com) has by far the biggest selection of shops, while other leading destinations include the Mall of the Emirates (www.malloftheemirates.com), Nakheel Mall (www.nakheelmall.ae) on The Palm and the very upmarket Marina Mall (www.marinamall.ae). Older venues include Burjuman (www.burjuman.com) in Bur Dubai, Festival Centre (www.dubaifestivalcitymall.com) in Festival City, and the sprawling downmarket Deira City Centre (www.deiracitycentre.com) in Garhoud. For a more unusual shopping experience, check out the faux-Italian Mercato (www.mercatoshoppingmall.com), the wacky Egyptian-themed Wafi (www.wafi.com) and the truly surreal Ibn Battuta Mall (www.ibnbattutamall.com).

Be prepared to bargain at the Gold Souk

WHAT TO BUY

Deira's famous Gold Souk is the focus of Dubai's roaring **gold** trade. Items are priced by weight according to the daily gold price, although bargaining is essential. The more upmarket Gold and Diamond Park (www.goldanddiamond-park.com) is another good place to shop for the precious metal, as well as diamonds, which sell here for significantly less than you'll pay back home.

There are **souvenir** shops in pretty much all the main malls. For traditional Arabian artefacts (coffeepots, shisha pipes, framed *khanjar* daggers and so on) look out for branches of Pride of Kashmir (www.prideofkashmir.com), while the more downmarket Al Jaber Gallery (www.aljabergallery.ae) offers a fun selection of cheap, cheerful and slightly cheesy mementoes. The best selection of souvenir shops can be found in Souk Madinat Jumeirah and Khan Murjan Souk – items for sale here are generally of a higher quality, albeit at above-average prices. The Camel Company (www.camelco.ae; branches in various malls citywide) does an entertaining line in cute toy camels and related merchandise, while Gallery One (www.g-1.com; also with outlets citywide) has a nice selection of limited-edition, Arabian-inspired artworks at relatively affordable prices.

Distinctive Arabian **perfumes** are available from Ajmal (www.ajmalperfume.com) and Arabian Oud (www.arabianoud.com),

NOTES

The month-long Dubai Shopping Festival (DSF; www.visitdubaishoppingfestival.com; Dec–Jan) was established in 1996 and now attracts around four million visitors annually, with shops across the city offering discounts and promotions, backed up by a lively programme of mall-based prize draws and entertainments. Dubai Summer Surprises (June–July) is another shopping-centred festival, with a similar range of discounts and in-mall entertainment designed to lure in punters during the hot summer months.

both with branches citywide. Alternatively, head for the Perfume Souk in Deira. Many places (including Ajmal) offer the chance to mix your own bespoke scents.

The citywide Carrefour supermarket chain is a great place to stock up on inexpensive local **food** and spices – halva, baklava, teas, nuts, spices, Arabian honey, Turkish coffee, saffron, caviar, *labneh* and olives. The Spice Souk in Deira is also good for spices (but bargain hard), while the citywide Bateel chain (www.bateel.com) dishes up a wide range of superior dates.

There are a few shops selling quality oriental **carpets** (including Emad Carpets in the Dubai Mall and several in the Deira Tower on Baniyas Square in Deira), although there's a far better selection (and lower prices) at the Blue Souk in Sharjah. Colourful Indian-style **fabrics** (plus Indian clothes) and pashminas are available in Bur Dubai Souk and the surrounding streets.

FESTIVALS AND EVENTS

January–February Emirates Airline Festival of Literature (www.emirateslitfest.com). The Middle East's largest literary festival, featuring leading local and international scribblers. Taste of Dubai (www.tasteofdubaifestival.com). Live cookery exhibitions in Dubai Media City by local and visiting international celebrity chefs, plus discounted food from many of the city's leading restaurants and chefs.
March–May Art Dubai (www.artdubai.ae). The biggest event in the Dubai visual arts calendar, with exhibits from galleries from around the world at Madinat Jumeirah. Sikka Art Festival (nine days in mid-March). Running concurrently with Art Dubai and other events, the Sikka Art Festival transforms Al Fahidi into a vibrant cultural district, with exhibitions, open-air film screenings, live music and more. Sharjah Biennial (www.sharjahbiennial.org). The oldest (established 1993) and most famous art festival in the Gulf (held in odd-numbered years only) showcasing major Arabian and international artists, along with other cultural events. Dubai Food Festival

(April–May). Citywide event with foodie bargains galore.

June–July Dubai Summer Surprises. A mainly mall-based event with a decent selection of shopping bargains masses of live children's entertainment.

September Dubai Fashion Week (www.dubaifashion-week.org). Leading local fashion event, showcasing work by designers from Arabia and beyond.

Celebrating Dubai's National Day

December Dubai International Film Festival (www.facebook.com/DubaiFilmFestival). International art house film screening, with a particular focus on home-grown work and usually a with few international celebs in attendance. National Day (Dec 2). The UAE's Independence Day is celebrated with parades, dhow races and performances of traditional music and dance. Al Dhafra Festival (www.bit.ly/DhafraFest; Dec–Jan). Held at the small town of Madinat Zayed in western Abu Dhabi emirate, this lively annual festival is devoted to traditional Bedouin desert culture and heritage, centred on a huge camel fair, alongside events showcasing the region's handicrafts, cooking and traditional date industry. Dubai Shopping Festival (Dec–Jan). Mall-based four-week shopping spectacular, while there are also lots of events at the Global Village in Dubailand (www.globalvillage.ae), with eye-catching international pavilions showcasing arts and crafts from around the world, as well as live music, dance and other events.

Food and drink

You won't go hungry in Dubai, and the city boasts a plethora of eating options of every conceivable type and in every price range. As you'd expect, the city is a particularly good place to sample Arabian cuisine, and there are also innumerable Indian restaurants, while just about every other style of global cuisine is available somewhere.

Much of the city's culinary reputation has been built on upscale fine dining in spectacular surroundings, attracting a long list of celebrity chefs over the years including luminaries such as Gordon Ramsay, Gary Rhodes, Heston Blumenthal, Nobu Matsuhisa, Vineet Bhatia, Pierre Gagnaire and Santi Santamaria. Dubai's status as the food capital of the Middle East was formally recognized with the publication in 2022 of the inaugural Michelin guide to the city, the first to any Middle Eastern destination, with eleven restaurants receiving Michelin stars.

Prices at the best places are predictably stratospheric, although those on a budget can still eat well for the equivalent of a few pounds/dollars at one of the city's streetside *shawarma* stands,

WHEN TO EAT – AND RAMADAN

Meals times in Dubai are what you'd expect in any international city. The only places with unusual timings are the city's more upscale Arabian restaurants, which often keep later hours, with diners often not arriving until 10pm or later and staying until well past midnight.

The one time of year when the opening hours vary from the norm is during the month of **Ramadan**, when Muslims fast during daylight hours, and non-Muslims are forbidden to eat, drink or smoke in public. Non-hotel restaurants are therefore closed until sunset (though some keep their kitchens open to serve take-aways), while diners in hotel restaurants are shielded from view behind wooden screens during the day, and no alcohol is served until sunset.

inexpensive Lebanese cafés or the hundreds of bargain-basement curry houses in Bur Dubai and Karama, while there are also several excellent and inexpensive seafood restaurants down the coast. Even if you've cash to burn it's still well worth eating with the locals to get a taste of the city's authentic ethnic eating scene. As leading local chef Stephen Flawith puts it, "Get off the beaten track and get into Karama, Bur Dubai and Deira. This is where the real magic happens."

Al Muntaha restaurant in the Burj Al Arab

Although much of the city's dining scene is still driven by five-star venues catering to image-conscious high-rollers, there's been a notable move in recent years towards more sustainable cuisine, with many restaurants now embracing planet-friendly practices (including three awarded the coveted Michelin "Green" star in 2022). There's also been a growing rediscovery of the region's cultural roots, with a growing number of traditional Emirati restaurants opening around the city, offering a range of local specialities which were almost impossible to find just a few years back.

WHERE TO EAT

Your basic choice when deciding where to eat boils down to a choice between the generally more upmarket, hotel-based restaurants, and the independent local cafés and smaller-scale restaurants (you'll

NOTES

The Dubai Friday brunch has long been a city institution, equivalent to the British Sunday roast, and particularly popular among the city's European expats. However, since the working week changed to Monday to Friday in 2022, Friday "brunch" is usually held on Friday evenings. Traditionally, restaurants lay on all-you-can-eat (and sometimes drink) deals. Check *Time Out Dubai* (www.timeoutdubai.com) for all the latest venues and deals – there are often deals for Saturday and Sunday brunches, too.

need to head to a hotel restaurant if you want to drink alcohol). The latter are obviously a lot cheaper, while the food is often as good as – if not better than – that served in much fancier hotel establishments. Just don't expect to get a glass of wine with your meal.

Hotel restaurants range from functional buffets through to some of the most extravagant dining destinations on the planet. Many of the best places take advantage of their spectacular locations with magical seafront restaurants (such as *Pierchic* at *Al Qasr* hotel and *Eauzone* at the *One&Only Royal Mirage*) and others atop the city's various skyscrapers (most notably *Al Muntaha* in the *Burj Al Arab* and *At.mosphere* in the Burj Khalifa).

Independent cafés and restaurants come in all sorts of forms. The old city is stuffed with down-at-heel, but often very good, Indian cafés, especially in Bur Dubai and Karama (try the "curry corridor" along Sheikh Zayed Road from just past the BurJuman Centre up to Karama). These divide into North Indian/Pakistani-style places serving hearty meat curries and pure-veg eateries dishing up good South Indian-style food, such as the excellent vegetarian *Saravanna Bhavan* chain (www.uae.saravanabhavan.com). There are also lots of low-key Arabian restaurants (particularly in Deira along Al Muraqqabat Rd – Dubai's "Little Iraq" – and parallel Al Rigga Rd). Deira also boasts plenty of Iranian kebab cafés and streetside shawarma joints.

Cafés further south in the newer parts of town tend to be more like their European equivalents (with prices to match). One place worth looking out for is *Zaatar w Zeit* (www.zaatarwzeit.net) chain, with has several branches citywide offering good Lebanese-style fast food at bargain prices. Affordable eats can also be found in the city's **malls**, all of which have a mix of cheap and cheerful international places (both local brands and international franchises, usually concentrated in dedicated food courts) alongside more upmarket restaurants scattered in strategic locations around the premises.

TOP 10 THINGS TO TRY

1. SHAWARMA

The ultimate meal-on-the-go, the classic shawarma is a little slice of rolled-up culinary heaven, served up by shawarma stands and cafés across Dubai, featuring fine cuts of succulent spit-roasted meat (chicken, beef or lamb), doused with sauce (ranging from garlic to tahini) and all wrapped in warm flatbread. The fastest and cheapest – not to mention one of the tastiest – things you'll eat anywhere in the city.

Shish kebab skewers

2. MEZZE

Lebanese-style mezze are Arabia's answer to tapas – a range of small dishes, served

DHOW DINNER CRUISES

For a meal with a difference, try one of the city's ever-popular dhow dinner cruises. Most cruises are either along the Creek or around the Dubai Marina, sailing in traditional replica wooden dhows and offering the chance to wine and dine on the water as your boat sails sedately between the souks or skyscrapers. Food tends to be fairly run-of-the mill: usually served buffet-style on cheaper tours (although more upmarket operators may offer a la carte), and there's usually live onboard entertainment of the Arabian music plus Russian belly dancer variety.

Operators change with bewildering rapidity and most lack even a reliable website – the best approach is to search and book online using latest reviews and any available discount deals. Reputable operators include Alexandra Dhow Cruise (www.dhowcruise.net), Marina Dhow Cruise Dubai (www.wmarinadhowcruisedubai.com), Al Mansour Dhow (www.mala.ae/al-mansour-dhow-cruise) and Bateaux Dubai (www.jaresortsholidays.com).

either hot or cold and offering contrasting textures and flavours, typically shared between a group. Classic mezze include *warak enab* (vine leaves stuffed with meat, akin to Greek dolmades), *fatayer* (crispy triangles of flatbread stuffed with spinach), *kibbeh* (fried minced lamb with crushed wheat), *sambousek* (samosa-style pastries filled with minced lamb and pine nuts or halloumi cheese or spinach), *arayes* (bread stuffed with minced lamb, tomato and cheese), *fattoush* (a green salad with toasted bread) and the sweet *kunafa* (spun pastry soaked in syrup and sprinkled with nuts, similar to baklava) – not to mention a host of other culinary stalwarts such as baba ganoush, hummous, tabbouleh and olives, all accompanied by giant mounds of piping-hot flatbread.

3. CAMEL MEAT

A classic Emirati dish, traditionally reserved for special occasions and important guests. It's still not widely served but can be found on the menu of some of the city's traditional restaurants if you look around. The taste is usually compared to beef, with a slightly gamey flavour, and the meat is typically slow-roasted and served alongside rice, although camel burgers are also increasingly popular.

4. MACHBOOS

A classic Gulf dish, machboos (also known as *kebsa*) is a popular dish and local take on the Indian biryani or Persian *polo*, with melt-in-the-mouth slow-cooked meat served on a bed of rice with tomatoes and onions, delicately flavoured with classic Arabian spice mixes such as *bezar*, an aromatic combination of cinnamon, ginger and cloves.

Enjoying traditional Arabian coffee

5. LUQAIMAT

Crunchy on the outside, soft and fluffy within, these miniature deep-fried dumplings (similar to the classic Indian *gulab jamun*) offer a mouthful of sweet-toothed indulgence, delicately flavoured with saffron and cardamom and then dipped in syrup or honey for the ultimate sugar rush.

6. BALALEET

This versatile local staple features a nest of delicately flavoured vermicelli noodles topped with an omelette, eaten hot or cold at any time of the day or night. The secret to balaleet is in the flavouring. Saffron and cardamom soaked in rose water are the key ingredients, with sugar added to give the vermicelli noodles their seductively contrasting hints of sweetness and spice.

Traditional baba ghanoush and fatayer bi sabanekh mezze

7. REGAG

Regag is the Gulf's answer to the European crêpe or the Indian dosa, comprising a delicate pancake packed with fillings ranging from meat or eggs through to cheese or vegetables. It also makes a good dessert when served with a drizzle of honey, or with a dash of thyme and labneh (Arabian-style yoghurt), a deliciously light and flavoursome snack on the go.

SHISHA PIPES

Shisha smoking, whether at the end of a meal or over a coffee, is a popular pastime amongst Dubai's sizeable community of expat Arabs. Shisha (aka as "hookah" or *nargileh*) are free-standing water pipes consisting of a water-filled container topped with tobacco, a small bowl of glowing charcoal and a long pipe with a mouthpiece.

Shisha tobacco can be smoked plain but is usually offered in a range of flavours – anything from apple, strawberry or melon through to fruit cocktail or cappuccino. Aficionados claim that because the smoke is drawn through water it is cleansed of much of its nicotine content. Even so, shisha can be habit-forming, although if you only sample it once or twice you're unlikely to become hooked on the hookah.

8. HAREES

The ultimate Gulf-style comfort food, harees features boiled, cracked or coarsely ground wheat, traditionally slow-cooked for hours with meat (chicken, lamb, beef or mutton) until it acquires its characteristic porridge-like consistency, after which it's served with a sprinkle of finely chopped herbs and topped with *dhnen kheneen* (Emirati-style clarified butter, or ghee).

9. MADROUBA

The home-spun "rice porridge" consists of meat, rice, milk and butter boiled down to a dense, sticky consistency and laced with warming spices – a carb- and protein-packed power-punch in a single bowl. The best places simmer their madrouba for hours to achieve the desired texture – significantly mushier than the perfect risotto, but every bit as good.

10. ARABIAN COFFEE

It's coffee, but not as you know it. Served in tiny, handleless cups, traditional Arabian coffee combines the caffeine punch of a triple

Lebanese kibbeh, a croquette stuffed with minced beef or lamb

espresso on steroids suffused with tantalizing hints of cardamom and cloves (but no milk or sugar).

DRINKING

Dubai's liberal outlook means that alcohol is readily available, although it doesn't come cheap, while licensed venues are almost exclusively limited to hotel-based bars and restaurants (plus night-clubs). There are basically two types of places to drink; English- or Irish-style **pubs** complete with traditional decor which wouldn't look out of place back in the British Isles, and swankier **bars**, including some memorably romantic venues in spectacular settings. For non-alcoholic drinks all the usual soft beverages can be found, along with plenty of fresh juices. And be sure to try some distinctive Arabian coffee, quite different to the Starbucks you'll be used to back home.

TO HELP YOU ORDER...

English is spoken absolutely everywhere, and English-language menus are universally available, so you're unlikely to have linguistic issues. However, we've included a few useful phrases below if you want to try out some Arabic while eating in one of the city's Emirati or Arabian restaurants.

Do you have a table? **Indaakum towla?**

Excuse me. **Afwan.**

I don't eat meat. **La akul lahem.**

What do you recommend? **Maatha tansah?**

May I have the bill, please? **Fatoura, laow samaht.**

I'd like … **Ana ureed…**

thank you **shukran**

yes **nam**

beef **lahem bakar**

bread **khobz**

chicken **dajaj**

coffee **kahwa**

fish **samak**

fruit **fawakah**

lamb **lahem harouf**

I've finished. **Ana khallast.**

no **la**

milk **haleeb**

rice **rouz**

salad **salata**

soup **shorba**

tea **shai**

vegetables **khodra**

water **mai**

... AND READ THE MENU

foul fava-bean stew with garlic and lemon

kofta minced lamb with parsley and onion

lahem meat (not including chicken)

logaimat fried balls made from egg, flour and saffron

mashawee grills

mehalabiya milk custard with pistachios and rosewater

salatat zatar thyme salad with onions, lemon and olive oil

shish kebab grilled mutton marinated with cumin and cinnamon

shish tawouq grilled chicken pieces marinated with cumin and cinnamon

Places to eat

The price categories below are based on the average cost of a meal for one with a glass of wine each in hotel venues, or soft drinks elsewhere.
$$$$ = Over 300dh
$$$ = Dhs150–300
$$ = Dhs75–150
$ = Less than Dhs75

BUR DUBAI

Al Fanar Al Seef, www.alfanarrestaurant.com/uae/al-seef. On the waterfront in the new Al Seef development, this faux-antique restaurant offers beautiful views from its breezy Creekside terrace alongside one of the old city's best seafood menus including traditional dishes like fish/shrimp *machboos* (rice dish) and *jesheed* (minced shark). **$$$**

Al Khayma Heritage Restaurant Al Fahidi, www.alkhayma.com. One of Dubai's best places to explore quality Middle Eastern and Gulf cuisine, with tasty breakfasts alongside salads, mezze and a good range of Arabian mains including traditional dishes like *machboos*. **$$$**

Arabian Tea House Café Al Fahidi, https://arabianteahouse.com. Lovely little café set in the idyllic courtyard of a traditional old house. The menu features a decent range of sandwiches and salads, plus assorted Arabian-style breakfasts, mezze and mains, and a good choice of juices and coffees. There's also a second branch located at the Jumeirah Archaeological Site. **$$**

XVA Café Al Fahidi www.xvahotel.com/café. Tucked away in an alley at the back of Al Fahidi Historical Neighbourhood, this shady courtyard café serves up good meat-free meals with a Middle Eastern or Indian twist, plus excellent breakfasts. **$$**

DEIRA

Al Bait Al Qadeem Old Baladiya Rd, www.albaitalqadeem.com. In a traditional Emirati building next to the Heritage House with a well-prepared menu and very reasonably priced regional dishes including various types of *machboos* and *goboli* (Gulf-style biryani), and *jeshid* (minced shark) along with more mainstream Lebanese-style kebabs. **$$**

KARAMA, OUD METHA, GARHOUD AND SATWA

Asha's Wafi, Oud Metha, www.ashasrestaurants.com. Owned by legendary Bollywood chanteuse Asha Bhosle, this smart Wafi restaurant offers Indian classics alongside more unusual regional specialities. **$$$**

Chhappan Bhog Sheikh Khalifa Bin Zayed Road (Trade Centre Road), Karama, https://chhappanbhog.me. Long-running Indian restaurant specializing in great veg *thalis* and other North and South Indian vegetarian fare. **$**

The Boardwalk Dubai Creek Golf and Yacht Club, Garhoud www.dubaigolf.com/dine. The mainstream menu of international food is tasty enough, but it's the terrific views from the outdoor Creekside seating on the restaurant's boardwalk which really steal the show. **$$$**

Khan Murjan Restaurant Souk Khan Murjan, Wafi www.wafi.com/souk. The centrepiece of the spectacular Khan Murjan Souk, this beautiful courtyard restaurant has proved a big hit with the city's Emiratis and expat Arabs thanks to the traditional atmosphere and unusually wide-ranging Middle Eastern menu, including unusual local Gulf dishes. **$$$**

Ravi's Near Satwa Roundabout, Satwa, www.facebook.com/ravirestaurantsuae. This legendary little café remains popular with locals, expats and tourists alike for its cheap and tasty Pakistani-style chicken, mutton and vegetable curries, while the outdoor seating offers a good (if noisy) perch from which to enjoy the passing street life. $

The Thai Kitchen Park Hyatt, Garhoud, www.bit.ly/ThaiKitchenDXB. Set on the *Park Hyatt*'s idyllic Creekside terrace, this is one of the best Thai restaurants in town, with a sumptuous range of classic Thai dishes. $$$$

SHEIKH ZAYED ROAD AND DOWNTOWN DUBAI

Armani Amal Armani Hotel, Downtown Dubai, www.armanihoteldubai.com. Inventive regional Indian cuisine with a European twist, plus spectacular views of the Dubai Fountain (ask for terrace seating). $$$$

At.mosphere Burj Khalifa, Downtown Dubai, www.atmosphereburjkhalifa.com. The world's highest restaurant, on the 122nd floor of the Burj Khalifa. You could choose a slightly less bank-breaking breakfast, or spectacular afternoon tea in the more laidback lounge. $$$$

Boca Gate Village 6, DIFC, www.boca.ae. One of only three Dubai restaurants to hold the coveted Michelin "Green" Star – awarded to places showing not only culinary excellence but also a real contribution to "sustainable gastronomy" – with a cool urban vibe and an inventive selection of Spanish-inspired tapas, plus good vegetarian options featuring desert plants foraged straight from the local desert and Hajar mountains. $$$

Thiptara The Palace hotel, Downtown Dubai, www.theaddress.com/en/restaurant/thiptara. Beautiful Thai restaurant set in a wooden pavilion jutting out into the waters by the Dubai Fountain. The menu offers sumptuous Bangkok-style seafood, plus meat and vegetarian options. $$$$

Time Out Market Souk al Bahar, Downtown Dubai, www.timeoutmarket.com/dubai. This innovative food court brings together a regularly changing array of local culinary talent from leading restaurants handpicked by the editors of the city's *Time Out* magazine, with seventeen different outlets and three bars, plus a breezy outdoor terrace, offering the chance to sample some of Dubai's best foodie offerings under a single roof, and at prices significantly below what you'll pay in the city's top restaurants. **$$$**

Zaroob Jumeirah Tower, Sheikh Zayed Rd, www.zaroob.com. This colourful café is a great place for wholesome Middle Eastern food, with a good selection of classics including assorted mezze, manakeesh, fatayer, falafel and shawarma. There's another branch in the Dubai Marina. **$$**

Zuma The Gate Village, DIFC, www.zumarestaurant.com. This über chic bar-restaurant is a hit both with Dubai's fashionistas and local foodies, thanks to its cool ambience and excellent range of Japanese fare. **$$$$**

JUMEIRAH

3 fils Jumeirah Fish Market, Jumeirah, www.3fils.com. Winner of the inaugural Best Restaurant in MENA award in 2022, *3 fils* has been wowing diners with its revolutionary combination of Michelin-standard cuisine served in a humble, café-like setting at giveaway prices. The menu focuses on Japanese seafood alongside a selection of more international-style meat offerings. No reservations accepted, so you'll likely have to queue. **$$**

Bu Qtair Fishing Harbour 2, Umm Suqeim. At the southern end of Kite Beach, this place started as a humble beach shack way back in the 1980s serving cheap food to local expat Indian workers and has stayed true to its roots and subcontinental flavours, with a choice of either fish or shrimps (there's no menu) doused in the café's signature masala marinade and then deep fried and served with rice, flaky parathas and a dab of curry sauce. **$**

Lime Tree Café Jumeirah Road, Jumeirah, www.thelimetreecafe.com. Set in an attractive modern villa, this neat café offers a classic slice of expat Jumeirah life. Healthy specialities include tasty wraps, delicious smoothies and arguably the best carrot cake in Dubai. **$$**

The Noodle House Madinat Jumeirah, www.jumeirah.com. Long-running Dubai favourite, this cheap(ish) and very cheerful noodle bar serves a great selection of Chinese and Southeast Asian food. **$$**

Pai Tai Al Qasr hotel, Madinat Jumeirah, www.jumeirah.com. One of the city's most romantic places to eat, with excellent Thai food plus live music and stunning views of the *Burj Al Arab* from the candlelit terrace. **$$$$**

Pierchic Al Qasr hotel, Madinat Jumeirah, www.jumeirah.com. Upmarket seafood restaurant in perhaps the most spectacular location of any restaurant in Dubai, at the end of a wooden pier with dreamy views of the Madinat Jumeirah and *Burj Al Arab* – particularly stunning after dark. **$$$$**

Ristorante L'Olivo at Al Mahara Burj Al Arab, Umm Suqeim, www.jumeirah.com. In the basement of the *Burj*, this is one of Dubai's oldest uber-deluxe restaurants: an intimate, low-lit space with tables arranged around a stunning circular aquarium – a bit like eating under the sea – with food overseen by Michelin-starred chef Andrea Migliaccio. **$$$$**

DUBAI MARINA AND THE PALM JUMEIRAH

Amala Jumeirah Zabeel Saray, The Palm Jumeirah, www.jumeirah.com. As opulently decorated as a Bollywood film set, Amala serves up a good range of mainly North Indian fare, all well prepared, and not too exorbitantly priced given the setting. **$$$$**

Buddha Bar Grosvenor House hotel, Dubai Marina, www.buddhabar.com. One of the most spectacular restaurants in Dubai, with a fine array of Japanese, Thai and Chinese mains. **$$$$**

Eauzone One&Only Royal Mirage hotel, Dubai Marina, www.royalmirage.oneandonlyresorts.com. Regularly voted the most romantic restaurant in Dubai, with a mainly Japanese menu and seating in little tents amid the beautifully floodlit waters of one of the hotel's swimming pools, which seems to transform by night into a luminous, palm-studded lagoon. **$$$$**

Indego by Vineet Grosvenor House hotel, Dubai Marina, www.indegobyvineet.com. Overseen by Vineet Bhatia, India's first Michelin-starred chef, this stylish restaurant showcases Bhatia's outstanding "contemporary Indian" cooking, with international ingredients and techniques. **$$$$**

Rhodes W1 Grosvenor House Hotel, Dubai Marina, www.rw1-dubai.com. Dubai outpost of the late UK celebrity chef Gary Rhodes, with a menu featuring succulent grills, steaks and seafood alongside British classics like fish 'n' chips with mushy peas and Manchester Scotch eggs. **$$$$**

Zheng He's Mina A'Salam, Madinat Jumeirah, www.jumeirah.com. One of the top Chinese restaurants in Dubai, with sumptuous decor, superb classic and contemporary Chinese fare and views from the beautiful *Burj*-facing terrace. **$$$$**

DRINKING

Bahri Bar Mina A'Salam Hotel, Madinat Jumeirah, www.madinatjumeirah.com. Superb little Arabian-style outdoor terrace, liberally scattered with canopied sofas, Moorish artefacts and Persian carpets, and offering gorgeous views of the *Burj* and Madinat Jumeirah – particularly lovely towards sunset.

Barasti Bar Le Méridien Mina Sehayi, Dubai Marina, www.barastieach.com. A consistently popular nightspot, this fun beachside bar is more or less always packed with an eclectic crowd of tourists and expats. Downstairs is more Ibiza-style chilled-out, with ambient music, shisha and loungers, while pubbier upstairs is generally noisier, with live DJs and a party atmosphere.

Chelsea Arms Pub Sheraton Dubai Creek Hotel, Deira, www.facebook.com/chelseaarmsdubai. Claiming to be the oldest pub in Dubai, this homely little boozer has been pulling pints since 1978 and now feels like a real piece of city history, complete with clunky wooden furniture, random Anglo memorabilia and a proper fireplace.

Double Decker Al Murooj complex, Sheikh Zayed Rd, www.facebook.com/DoubleDeckerDubai. One of the liveliest pubs in town, with quirky decor themed after the old London Routemaster buses and usually busy with a more-than-averagely tanked-up crowd of expats and western tourists. Live music and/or DJ most nights from around 9pm.

Fibber Magee's Sheikh Zayed Rd, www.fibbersdubai.com. One of the city's best-kept secrets, and Dubai's most successful stab at a traditional Irish pub, with convincingly authentic wood-beamed interior and a good selection of draught tipples. There's also regular live music and good, homely pub food.

The Golden Lion Port Rashid, Bur Dubai, www.qe2.com. Classic old-school British drinking establishment aboard the famous *QE2* cruise liner with an assortment of clunky wooden tables and plush velvet velour, although the main attraction is obviously the chance to sup aboard this historic old vessel.

Rooftop Terrace One&Only Royal Mirage hotel, Dubai Marina, www.royalmirage.oneandonlyresorts.com. On the roof of the *Royal Mirage*, this is one of Dubai's most stylish and romantic spots to drink, with seductive Moorish decor, cushion-strewn pavilions, silver-tray tables and other assorted Arabian artefacts.

Skyview Bar Burj al Arab, Umm Suqeim, www.burjalarab.com. Landmark bar perched near the summit of the *Burj Al Arab*, with colourful psychedelic decor and vast sea views. You'll need to reserve in advance via email at BAArestaurants@jumeirah.com.

Travel essentials

PRACTICAL INFORMATION

ACCESSIBLE TRAVEL

Dubai is one of the Middle East's most accessible destinations. Most of the upmarket hotels have specially adapted rooms for disabled travellers, and some malls include accessible parking spaces and specially equipped toilets. Transport is also fairly well adapted. Dubai Taxi (tel: 04 208 0000; www.dubaitaxi.ae) has vehicles equipped with ramps and lifts, while the Metro features tactile guide paths, lifts and ramps to assist visually- and mobility-impaired visitors, as well as wheelchair spaces in all compartments. The city's waterbuses can also be used by mobility-impaired visitors, and staff will assist you, while there are also dedicated facilities at the airport. Sadly, most of the city's older heritage buildings are not accessible.

ACCOMMODATION

There's a huge range of accommodation in Dubai, including innumerable five-star hotels, although good accommodation lower down the price scale is more difficult to find. The cheapest accommodation is the one- and two-star hotels around the old city centre in Bur Dubai and Deira, although even here you'll struggle to find a room for less than US$50 a night. Mid-range places start at around US$100 per night, while rates at the city's more upmarket hotels start at around US$200 a night, rising to as much as US$2000 a night and more. For beach hotels it pays to reserve as far ahead as possible.

Dubai's high season runs roughly from October through to April. The low season stretches through the hotter months of May to August, during which prices usually fall significantly. Booking online you'll find an absolutely vast selection of places to choose from, but be aware that many lower- and mid-range places pimp their photos shamelessly. Don't be fooled by shiny images of marbled foyers and fancy rooms, and check reviews thoroughly before committing.

AIRPORTS

Dubai International Airport (airport code DXB; www.dubaiairports.ae), is centrally located in Garhoud around 7km from the old city centre.

There are three terminals. Terminal 3 is where all Emirates flights arrive and depart. Terminal 1 handles other long-haul international flights, while Terminal 2 handles short-haul flights. Both Terminals 1 and 3 have their own dedicated metro stations, and there are plentiful taxis, although note that these charge a Dhs 20 surcharge when picking up from the airport. A tiny handful of flights land at the new **Al Maktoum International Airport** (airport code DWC), in the far south of the city.

ALCOHOL

Dubai has a relatively liberal attitude to the consumption of alcohol by non-Muslims, although it's only available in bars and fancier restaurants, almost all of which are attached to the city's larger hotels. Alcohol is not sold in supermarkets and only residents with government-issued liquor licences can buy from the two local licensed vendors.

Dubai has a zero-tolerance approach to drink-driving and if you're caught driving with even the merest suggestion of alcohol in your system you're likely to face time in jail. Note that you risk arrest if, driving the morning after a heavy night out, there is still any trace of alcohol in your blood. Being drunk and disorderly in public is also an offence, as is buying alcohol for a Muslim. The sale of alcohol everywhere is restricted during the Islamic holy month of Ramadan.

APPS

International taxi apps such as the Dubai-based Careem (www.careem.com) and Uber (www.uber.com) are available, as well as Hala (www.halaride.com). See page 137 under "Public transport" for more information.

BUDGETING FOR YOUR TRIP

Dubai is generally an expensive destination, although eating out in cheaper restaurants and travelling around using public transport are both refreshingly affordable.

Accommodation. A standard double room costs around US$50–60 per night in basic a one-star hotel and from around $80 to $130 in most mid-range places. More upmarket hotels start from around $200 per night, with rates rising north of $1,000 in the city's most luxurious establishments. Hotel prices often tumble spectacularly during the hot summer months (May–Sept), although you won't want to venture far from a/c.

Meals and drinks. It's possible to eat cheaply if you're happy with no-frills dining, and the food can still be very good. A streetside *shawarma* wrap will cost just a couple of dollars, while a curry in a no-nonsense Indian or Pakistani café will cost around $5–10. Main courses in most decent Western-style restaurants go for around $15–20, while for fine dining mains are likely to cost $30 and up. Soft drinks cost similar to those in the west. Alcoholic drinks will ramp up the bill considerably. Beer costs a bit more than in the West, while prices for fine wines and spirits can be stratospheric.

Local transport. Transport is cheap if you stick to public transport: tickets on the Dubai Metro, buses and trams start from Dhs4, while a daily tourist pass costs just Dh22 (US$6), giving unlimited use of the city's public transport, which reaches just about every part of the city you're likely to want to go. Taxis are reasonably priced, too, with a minimum charge of Dhs12 and a cost of around Dhs2 per kilometre (although taxis picked up at the airport have a Dhs20 surcharge).

Entrance charges. Along with accommodation, admission charges are likely to be your biggest expenses. Tickets to government-run heritage sites, museums and parks are relatively modest (usually just a few dollars, rising to a maximum of around $14 at the landmark new Al Shindagha Museum). Conversely, entrance fees to privately run attractions are generally pricey. Tickets to the observation deck of the Burj Khalifa, for example, cost from $50 and up, while entrance fees to family attractions like the city's waterparks can easily top US$200 for a family of four.

CHILDREN

Childcare facilities are on a par with those in the West. Most malls have changing facilities in the women's public toilets; many also have supervised indoor play areas. Many of the more upmarket beach resorts have kids' club and babysitting services.

CRIME AND SAFETY

Dubai is generally a pretty safe place. It pays to take all the usual precautions, but instances of theft or pickpocketing are remarkably rare for such a large city and there is no part of the metropolis in which you are likely to feel unsafe, even late at night. You're actually much more likely to fall foul of the law yourself in Dubai than to be the victim of crime, and foreign visitors are regularly arrested for a wide range of offences. These include possession of drugs (even in microscopic quantities, or in one's bloodstream on arrival) and traffic-related offences (drink-driving particularly), through to apparently harmless actions such as kissing in public or gesturing at fellow motorists. Homosexuality is also illegal, although prosecution of Westerners is extremely rare.

CUSTOMS AND ENTRY REQUIREMENTS

Free thirty-day visas are available on arrival at the airport for nationals of the UK, Ireland and most other Western European countries, the US, Canada, Australia and New Zealand and selected Asian countries. Visas can be extended for 600dh online at www.gdrfad.gov.ae/en.

Visitors are allowed to bring in up to four hundred cigarettes (or fifty cigars or 500g of tobacco), four litres of alcohol (or two 24-can cases of beer), and cash and travellers' cheques up to a value of 40,000dh. Prohibited items include drugs, pornographic material, material offensive to Islamic teachings, non-Islamic religious propaganda and evangelical literature. Note that many drugs available over the counter or on prescription in the West are illegal in Dubai. Check in advance if you are planning on bringing any medicines with you, and get a doctor's certificate if in doubt.

DRIVING

Given how good public transport is in Dubai there's really no incentive to hire a car unless you're venturing out of the city. Driving in Dubai isn't for the fainthearted thanks to heavy traffic, aggressive driving styles and navigational difficulties. If you don't know your way around, a real-time-enabled navigational app is essential. It's also crucial to remember that you can be jailed for "offensive" hand gestures in the UAE. Do not under any circumstances remonstrate when you get viciously cut up or aggressively tailgated, as you will be. Accidents are common (the main roads between Dubai and Al Ain and Abu Dhabi are particularly notorious) and surveillance doesn't seem to deter kamikaze high-speed driving. If you are involved in an accident, stop and wait for the police and do not move your vehicle. A police report on every level of accident is required for insurance claims. If you are stopped by police, you must be able to produce your driving licence and car hire/insurance papers (originals, not copies). And do not under any circumstances attempt to hire a 4WD and go off into the desert unless you're an experienced off-road driver.

If you do still decide to hire a car, all the usual companies can be found including **Avis** (www.avis.ae), **Budget** (www.budget-uae.com), **Thrifty** (www.thriftyuae.com), **Europcar** (www.europcardubai.com), **Hertz** (www.hertz.ae) and **Sixt** (www.sixt.ae). The cheapest cars start from under $40 a day. Most national driving licences are recognised for hire purposes.

ELECTRICITY

The mains electricity in Dubai is 220–240 volts AC meaning that UK appliances will work directly off the mains supply, although US appliances may need a transformer. Wall sockets are designed for British-type three-pin plugs. Adaptors for two-pin appliances are available in supermarkets.

EMBASSIES AND CONSULATES

As Abu Dhabi, not Dubai, is the federal capital of the UAE, Dubai tends to have foreign consulates, rather than embassies. Contact your consulate only for real emergencies, such as loss of a passport or all your money, a serious accident or trouble with the police. Details for selected countries are:

UK Al Seef Rd, Bur Dubai tel: 04 309 4444, www.gov.uk/world/united-arab-emirates.

US Consulate-General, Corner of Al Seef Rd and Sheikh Khalifa bin Zayed Rd, Bur Dubai tel: 04 309 4000, www.https://ae.usembassy.gov.

EMERGENCIES

Dial 999 for police or ambulance, or 997 for fire.

ETIQUETTE

Although the UAE is very liberal compared with other Gulf states, it is still a conservative Muslim country and visitors should respect this. Clothing that is acceptable in a nightclub or on a beach is not appropriate for the city's daytime streets (although you'll likely see many expats flaunting these rules). As a general rule of thumb, it's best to cover your upper arms, while women are expected to wear below-the-knee skirts or trousers. It's ok for men to wear shorts, although to local Emiratis it looks like you're walking around in your underwear.

During the holy month of Ramadan do not eat, smoke or drink in public.

GETTING THERE

Most visitors arrive at Dubai International Airport, though cruise ships dock at Dubai Cruise Terminal in Port Rashid. Alternatively, it's possible to fly into the neighbouring emirates of Abu Dhabi and Sharjah and cross into Dubai by road, or to travel overland from neighbouring Oman.

Dubai's International Airport (www.dubaiairports.ae) is the major Gulf hub for international air travel, with numerous connections worldwide. There are currently nonstop flights to Dubai from London Heathrow with Emirates, British Airways, Virgin and Royal Brunei Airlines, and numerous one-stop options with several European and Asian carriers and also with Etihad, Qatar Airways and Gulf Air. Emirates also fly nonstop to Dubai from some regional UK airports. From the US, there are a few nonstop flights with Emirates, plus one-stop options with a range of other North American carriers. The flying time from London to Dubai, direct, is about seven hours.

HEALTH AND MEDICAL CARE

There are virtually no serious health risks in Dubai (unless you include the traffic). The city is well equipped with modern hospitals, while all four- and five-star hotels have English-speaking doctors on call 24hr. Tap water is safe to drink, while even the city's cheapest curry houses and shawarma cafés maintain good standards of food hygiene. The only possible health concern is the heat. Summer temperatures regularly climb into the mid-forties, making sunburn, heatstroke and acute dehydration a real possibility. Stay in the shade, and drink lots of water.

There are pharmacies all over the city, including a number run by the BinSina chain (www.binsina.ae) which are open 24hr. The number to dial for an **ambulance** is 999. There are good government hospitals as well as numerous private clinics. The main emergency hospital is the government-run Rashid Hospital (tel: 04 219 2000) near Maktoum Bridge in Bur Dubai. Dental problems can be dealt with by the American Dental Clinic (www.americandentalclinic.com) or My Dental Clinic (tel: 04 338 8939, www.mydentalclinic.ae).

LANGUAGE

Arabic is the official language of the UAE, but English is spoken by just about everyone, usually to a high standard, and you'll have absolutely no problems in getting by without a single word in any of the myriad other languages spoken in the city by the various expat communities (of which Arabic, Hindi, Urdu, Malayalam and Tagalog are amongst the most common). Having said that, if you are lucky enough to meet local Emiratis they will always appreciate any attempts to communicate in Arabic, even if it's only a stock greeting.

hello **marhaba**
welcome **ahlan wa-sahlan (ahlan)**
peace be with you (greeting) **as-salaam alaykum**
and with you be peace (response) **wa-alaykum as-salaam**
good morning **sabah al khayr**
good morning (response) **sabah al nour**
good evening **masaa al khayr**
good evening (response) **masaa al nour**
My name is… **ana ismi…**
What is your name? **shou ismac?**
How are you? **kayf haalak?**
well **zayn**

please **min fadlak**
thank you **shukran**
yes/no **naam/la**
finished (as in I have … or it is …) **khallas**
goodbye, peace be with you **maa as-salaama**

LGBTQ+ TRAVELLERS

Dubai is one of the world's less-friendly LGBTQ+ destinations. Homosexuality is illegal under UAE law, with punishments of up to ten years in prison, even if prosecutions of foreigners are extremely rare. Despite this, the city boasts a very clandestine LGBTQ+ scene, attracting both foreigners and Arabs from even less permissive cities around the Gulf, although you'll need to hunt hard to find it without local contacts. Relevant websites are routinely censored within the UAE, so you'll probably have to do your online research before you arrive.

MONEY

The currency in Dubai is the UAE dirham (usually abbreviated "Dh" or "AED"), which is pegged to the US dollar at the rate of Dhs3.6731 to US$1. There are 100 fils in a dirham. The notes in circulation are currently Dhs 5, 10, 20, 50, 100, 200, 500 and 1000.

Banks are generally open Mon–Sat from 8am to 2pm, although some may close for a period on Friday for prayers. The best places to change foreign currency and traveller's cheques into dirhams are the numerous exchanges found in malls and souks, which keep shop hours. The main chains are Al Ansari Exchange (www.alansariexchange.com), Al Fardan Exchange (www.alfardanexchange.com) and Thomas Cook Al Rostamani (www.alrostamaniexchange.com). Hotels may exchange cash and traveller's cheques for guests, although rates are likely to be poor.

Major international credit and debit cards are accepted in large shops, most restaurants and just about all hotels. When shopping in souks, it's better to bargain for the "best price" with cash.

OPENING HOURS

Until recently, Dubai (and the rest of the UAE) ran on an Islamic rather than a Western schedule, with the city operating according to a basic five-day working week running Sunday to Thursday, with Friday as the Islamic holy day and Friday and Saturday as the "weekend". All this changed on January 1, 2022, when the government officially adopted the Western Saturday–Sunday weekend, with most private companies swiftly following suit, although a few places still remain closed on Friday mornings.

Shops in malls generally open daily from 10am to 10pm, and until midnight on Friday and Saturday (and sometimes Thursday as well); shops in souks follow a similar pattern, though many places close for a siesta between around 1–4pm depending on the whim of the owner. Most restaurants open daily for lunch and dinner (although some more upmarket hotel restaurants open for dinner only). Pubs tend to open daily from around noon until 2am; bars from around 6pm until 2/3am.

PHOTOGRAPHY

Dubai is a very photogenic city, although the often harsh desert light can play havoc with colour and contrast – for the best results head out between around 7am and 9am in the morning, or after 4pm.

It's worth noting that many upmarket hotels and restaurants are extremely sniffy about people taking photographs of their establishments, particularly if other guests are around. Outside, things are more relaxed, although obviously it's polite to ask before you take photos of people, and you risk causing considerable offence (or worse) if you shove your lens in the face of local Emiratis – ladies in particular – without permission. And don't take pictures of anything that might be considered a sensitive location including police stations, government buildings and royal palaces.

POST OFFICES

The two most convenient post offices for visitors are the Al Musalla Post Office at Al Fahidi Roundabout, and the Deira Post Office on Al Sabkha Road, near the intersection with Baniyas Road.

PUBLIC HOLIDAYS

There are eight public holidays in Dubai: three fall on fixed dates, while the others shift annually year-on-year according to the Islamic calendar, shifting by (usually) 11 days each year.

Fixed dates

New Year's Day **Jan 1**

Commemoration Day (Martyrs' Day) **Nov 30**

UAE National Day **Dec 2**

Moveable holidays

Milad un Nabi (Prophet Mohammed's Birthday)

Eid ul Fitr (end of Ramadan)

Arafat Day (beginning of the pilgrimage to Mecca)

Eid al Adha (Feast of the Sacrifice)

Al Hijra (Islamic New Year)

PUBLIC TRANSPORT

Almost all public transport in Dubai – metro, buses and waterbuses (but not *abras*) is covered by the **Nol** integrated ticket system (www.nol.ae). You will need to get a pre-paid Nol card before you can use any of these; no tickets are sold on board. Cards can be bought (or topped up) at any metro station and at numerous bus stops. **Fares** are based how many of Dubai's seven travel zones you pass through, ranging from 4dh up to a maximum of 8.50dh for a single trip (8–17dh in Gold Class).

There are two main types of Nol card; all are valid for five years and can store up to 1000dh worth of credit. The **Silver Card** costs 25dh (including 19dh credit). The **Gold Card** (same price) is almost identical, but allows users to travel on Gold Class compartments on the metro.

An alternative is the **Red Ticket** (a paper ticket, rather than a plastic card). This has been specifically designed for tourists, costs just 2dh and is valid for 90 days. The main benefit of the Red Ticket is that it allows you to purchase a useful one-day pass (22/44dh in regular/Gold class), valid citywide, although you'll have to recharge the ticket for each journey (up to a maximum of five recharges).

Dubai's **metro** system (www.rta.ae) now covers much of the city, with state-of-the-art driverless trains running on a mixture of underground and overground lines, and eye-catching modern stations. There are two lines. The 67km-long **Red Line** starts near the airport and then runs south down Sheikh Zayed Road to the far south of the city (with a branch line splitting off to the Expo 2020 site). The 22km-long **Green Line** arcs around the city centre, running from north of the airport, via Deira and Bur Dubai and then down to the Creek at Jaddaf.

Trains run roughly every 5–9 minutes, with services operating Mon–Sat from around 5am until midnight (until 1am on Fri) and on Sundays from 8am to 1am. **Fares** are calculated according to the distance travelled, ranging from 4dh up to a maximum of 8.5dh for a single trip (or 8–17dh in Gold Class; see below), or 22dh for an entire day's travel (44dh in Gold Class) using a Nol Red Ticket (see above). Children under 5 or shorter than 0.9m travel free. Note that tickets are sold at the information kiosks located at the departure gates in all stations in the event that the actual ticket office is shut (as they often are). Be aware that the names of metro stations are commercially sponsored and change with maddening and baffling regularity, so don't be surprised if the same station is referred to by two or more different names.

All trains have a Gold Class compartment at the front or back of the train (look for the signs above the platform barriers) costing double the standard fare. These have slightly plusher seating and decor, although the main benefit is that they're usually fairly empty, meaning that you're pretty much guaranteed a seat, a real bonus given how packed ordinary-class carriages often are – plus you'll get the best views since you're right at the end of the train. All trains also carry a dedicated carriage for women and children next to the Gold Class compartment. Again, these are usually less crowded than ordinary-class carriages.

Down in the southern city, the small **Dubai Tram** network offers a convenient (if not particularly fast) way of getting around the Marina and Umm Suqeim. The network links seamlessly with the metro (with interconnecting stations at DMCC/Jumeirah Lakes Towers and Sobha Realty/Dubai Marina) and also the Palm Monorail. Fares are covered by the Nol system and all trams have Gold Class and women-and-children-only carriages. Operating hours are Mon–Sat 6am–1am and Sunday 9am–1am, with departures every 8min.

Dubai has an extensive and efficient **bus** network (www.bit.ly/BusDXB), though most routes cover parts of the city that casual visitors are unlikely to want to reach. The majority of services originate or terminate at either the Gold Souk Bus Station in Deira or Al Ghubaiba Bus Station in Bur Dubai (many services call at both). Bus stops are clearly signed, some also air-conditioned; you'll also find a useful map of the bus network inside each shelter.

For visitors, the most useful service is bus #8 (roughly every 20min), which runs from the Gold Souk station to Al Ghubaiba and then due south, down Jumeirah Road to the *Burj al Arab* and Dubai Marina, covering a big chunk of the city not served by the metro or tram (although if you're heading to the southern city from the old centre it's quicker to take the metro to the nearest jumping-off point, and then a cab or tram for the last part of your journey).

Away from areas served by the metro and tram, **taxis** offer the quickest and most convenient way of getting around. These are most easily booked through one of the various apps covering the city including Uber, Careem and Hala (a joint collaboration between Careem and the government's RTA department), and can also be booked on the central booking number: 04 208 0808. Large malls and big hotels are also generally good places to pick up a cab; if not, just stand on the street and wave at anything that passes.

Fares for rides booked through Uber and Careem are generally a bit cheaper than those in traditional cabs, but are pretty good value whoever you travel with. Traditional cabs cost a basic 1.71dh per kilometre (minimum charge 12dh, or 25dh from the airport). Booking by phone adds an extra 3dh to the fare (or 5.50dh from 10pm to 6am). If you want a taxi to wait for you, it costs 0.5dh per minute. You'll also have to pay a 4dh surcharge if your taxi travels through a Salik tollgate.

For all Dubai's sleek modern transport infrastructure, the easiest way of crossing the Creek is still by hopping aboard one of the quaint little wooden boats – or **abras** – which ferry passengers between Deira and Bur Dubai. There are two main abra routes: from Deira Old Souk Abra Station to Bur Dubai Abra Station, and (slightly further down the Creek) from Al Sabkha

Abra Station to Bur Dubai Old Souk Abra Station. The fare is just 1dh (under 5s free). Boats leave as soon as full (meaning, in practice, every couple of minutes, except late at night), and the crossing takes about five minutes.

An alternative to the traditional abra is the slightly fancier and more comfortable "petrol heritage abra". Trips cost 2dh and boats run the two routes above along with two additional routes further south along the Creek connecting Al Fahidi and Al Seef on the Bur Dubai side with Baniyas in Deira.

Down in Dubai Marina, more modern a/c abras (aka waterbuses) also connect Marina Mall and Marina Walk (daily noon to 11pm, Fri–Sun until midnight; 5dh), while additional evening services (daily 4–11.30pm) criss-cross the Dubai Marina, with stops including Marina Mall, Marina Walk, Marina Promenade and Bluewaters Island (3dh, or 11dh to Bluewaters). Modern abras also run between Jaddaf and Festival City (a/c abras: daily 8am–11.30pm; "petrol heritage" abras Sat & Sun 4–11.20pm), while a weekend-only "petrol heritage" abra service connects Jaddaf, Festival City and Dubai Creek Harbour (near Ras al Khor; Sat & Sun 4–11.20pm). You'll also find on-demand abra cruises available on the Dubai Water Canal (see page 69).

Further memorable views of Dubai from the water can be had by taking a ride on the smart, modern **Dubai Ferry**. Services run between Al Ghubaiba in Bur Dubai and Dubai Marina, sailing around the outside of the Palm en route and with stops at the entrance to the Dubai Canal in Jumeirah and at Bluewaters Island and Marina Mall in the Marina itself. There are currently two services daily in each direction, leaving early afternoon and early evening and costing 50dh; the journey from Bur Dubai to the Marina takes around 2hr. There's also a twice-daily sightseeing round trip (75dh) from the Marina to the *Atlantis* resort on the Palm (although the boat doesn't actually stop at *Atlantis*). Check the latest details at www.rta.ae, since tours and timings change frequently.

If you want to grab your own boat, check out the city's **water taxi** service, using swanky modern a/c vessels seating around ten people. Rides can be booked between any of the forty water-taxi stations dotted around the city (tel: 800 90 90, email: WTbook@rta.ae).

RELIGION

Islam is the official religion of the UAE, but there is freedom of worship for Christians in church compounds, on the understanding that they do not proselytize. All Muslims, except young children, the elderly and pregnant women, observe Ramadan, which lasts 29 or 30 days each year. During this month they abstain from food and drink (and smoking and sex) from sunrise to sunset. Most hotel restaurants will serve food to visitors during the daytime (often screening tables from public view) but you should be sensitive not to eat or drink (or chew gum) in public during this holy month. The dates for Ramadan move each year, following the Islamic calendar.

TELEPHONE

The international dialling code for the UAE is 971. The code for Dubai landlines is 04 – overseas callers should drop the 0. The code for UAE mobile phones is 050, 055 or 056 – again, overseas callers should drop the first 0. Free local SIM cards are now handed out to all tourists on arrival, pre-charged with a modest amount of credit and easily topped up online (following the enclosed instructions) offering cheap data plus inexpensive local and international calls.

TIME ZONE

Dubai is four hours ahead of GMT (UCT), throughout the year.

New York	London	Jo'burg	**Dubai**	Sydney	Auckland
3am	8am	10am	**noon**	7pm	9pm

TIPPING

Tipping is appreciated, but not expected. A 10 percent service charge is often added automatically to bills, although this is not necessarily shared with staff – better to leave cash if you wish to express your appreciation. Tipping in taxis is not expected, although many visitors often round up the fare and let the driver keep the change.

TOURS

A number of companies run **city sightseeing tours** combining the main heritage sights with striking modern architecture. Hop-on, hop-off tours are available with the Big Bus Company (www.bigbustours.com)

Some of the city's most interesting cultural experiences can be arranged through the **Sheikh Mohammed Centre for Cultural Understanding** (www.cultures.ae). The centre runs **walking tours** of Al Fahidi, plus excellent tours of Jumeirah Mosque and other activities including Gulf Arabic classes and "cultural breakfasts", offering a rare chance to interact at length with local Emiratis. Insightful foodie tours of the old city are run by **Frying Pan Adventures** (www.fryingpanadventures.com), getting off the tourist trail and diving into all sorts of handpicked local eating places.

Other tours include desert safaris, dhow cruises and tours of neighbouring emirates, as well as other activities from fishing trips to helicopter rides. The leading local tour company is Arabian Adventures (www.arabian-adventures.com). Other reliable operators include Lama Tours (www.lamadubai.com) and Orient Tours (www.orienttours.ae), while more interesting bespoke tours can be arranged through Platinum Heritage Luxury Tours (www.platinum-heritage.com) and Knight Tours (www.facebook.com/knighttoursdubai), including small-group desert safaris in vintage Land Rovers. For details on tour operators for specific activities, see page 98.

WEBSITES AND INTERNET ACCESS

www.visitdubai.com The emirate's main tourist website.

www.visitabudhabi.ae Official site of the Abu Dhabi Tourism Authority and a great resource for info on the emirate's lesser-known attractions.

www.timeoutdubai.com Latest listings and reviews of what's on in the city.

www.thenational.ae The UAE's leading English-language newspaper.

www.detainedindubai.org This website might make you decide you don't actually want to go to the UAE after all, with comprehensive coverage of the country's murky legal processes and assorted miscarriages of justice, plus regularly updated reports on the current plight of the many expats locked up on the flimsiest of pretexts.

Index

THE **MINI** ROUGH GUIDE TO **DUBAI**

First Edition 2025

Editor: Libby Davies
Author: Gavin Thomas
Picture Editor: Piotr Kala
Picture Manager: Tom Smyth
Cartography Update: Carte
Layout: Pradeep Thapliyal
Production Operations Manager: Katie Benett
Publishing Technology Manager: Rebeka Davies
Head of Publishing: Sarah Clark
Photography Credits: Apa Publications 23, 25, 27, 38, 87; Chris Bradley/ Apa Publications 15M, 89; Dubai Tourism 15, 16ML, 71, 73, 109; iStock 10, 14MC, 14TL, 15T, 16MC, 34, 40, 43, 47, 51, 53, 58, 61, 65, 74, 77, 90, 92, 96, 100, 111, 114, 116; Kevin Cummins/Apa Publications 16TL, 48, 98, 104; Shutterstock 1, 4, 5, 6, 8, 12, 14MC, 14TC, 14ML, 14TL, 15M, 16ML, 18TL, 18ML, 18MC, 18ML, 20TL, 20ML, 20MC, 20ML, 29, 30, 32, 36, 45, 55, 57, 63, 67, 68, 79, 81, 83, 85, 94, 102, 107, 113
Cover Credits: Dubai skyline **Shutterstock**

About the author

Gavin Thomas has been visiting Dubai for over twenty years and has been privileged to witness at first hand the most recent chapters in the city's astonishing transformation from Gulf backwater to global metropolis. During that time he's watched the city quadruple in size, seen the Dubai Marina transform from empty desert into a forest of skyscrapers and observed the Burj Khalifa emerge magically out of a very large hole in the ground. Other writing credits include the Rough Guides to Oman, Sri Lanka, Rajasthan, Myanmar and Cambodia.

Distribution

UK, Ireland and Europe: Apa Publications (UK) Ltd; sales@roughguides.com
United States and Canada: Ingram Publisher Services; ips@ingramcontent.com
Australia and New Zealand: Booktopia; retailer@booktopia.com.au
Worldwide: Apa Publications (UK) Ltd; sales@roughguides.com

Special Sales, Content Licensing and CoPublishing

Rough Guides can be purchased in bulk quantities at discounted prices. We can create special editions, personalised jackets and corporate imprints tailored to your needs. sales@roughguides.com; http://roughguides.com

Printed in Czech Republic

This book was produced using **Typefi** automated publishing software.

Contact us

Every effort has been made to provide accurate information in this publication, but changes are inevitable. The publisher cannot be held responsible for any resulting loss, inconvenience or injury sustained by any traveller as a result of information or advice contained in the guide. We would appreciate it if readers would call our attention to any errors or outdated information, or if you feel we've left something out. Please send your comments with the subject line "Rough Guide Mini Dubai Update" to mail@uk.roughguides.com.

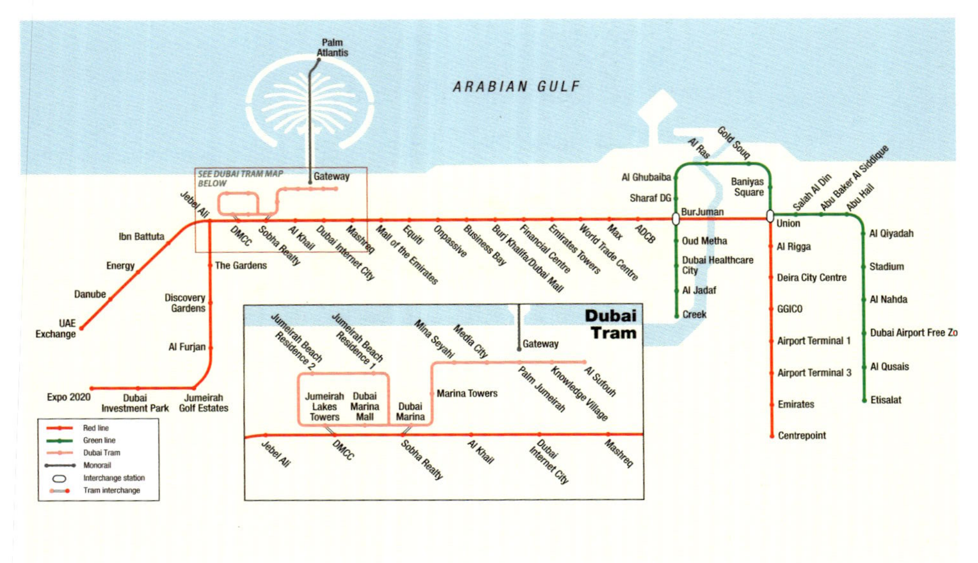
ARABIAN GULF
Palm Atlantis
SEE DUBAI TRAM MAP BELOW
Gateway
Jebel Ali
DMCC
Sobha Realty
Al Khail
Dubai Internet City
Mashreq
Mall of the Emirates
Equiti
Onpassive
Business Bay
Burj Khalifa/Dubai Mall
Financial Centre
Emirates Towers
World Trade Centre
Max
ADCB
BurJuman
Union
Ibn Battuta
Energy
Danube
UAE Exchange
The Gardens
Discovery Gardens
Al Furjan
Jumeirah Golf Estates
Dubai Investment Park
Expo 2020
Al Ghubaiba
Sharaf DG
Al Ras
Gold Souq
Baniyas Square
Oud Metha
Dubai Healthcare City
Al Jadaf
Creek
Salah Al Din
Abu Baker Al Siddique
Abu Hail
Al Qiyadah
Stadium
Al Nahda
Dubai Airport Free Zo
Al Qusais
Etisalat
Al Rigga
Deira City Centre
GGICO
Airport Terminal 1
Airport Terminal 3
Emirates
Centrepoint
Dubai Tram
Jumeirah Beach Residence 2
Jumeirah Beach Residence 1
Mina Seyahi
Media City
Gateway
Al Sufouh
Knowledge Village
Palm Jumeirah
Marina Towers
Jumeirah Lakes Towers
Dubai Marina Mall
Dubai Marina
Jebel Ali
DMCC
Sobha Realty
Al Khail
Dubai Internet City
Mashreq
Red line
Green line
Dubai Tram
Monorail
Interchange station
Tram interchange